Dearest Mother

My fondest love

Richard

Natter Natter

Natter Natter
RICHARD BRIERS

Cartoons by Larry

Good Luck

Richard Briers

J M Dent & Sons Ltd
London Melbourne Toronto

First published 1981
© Richard Briers 1981
Illustrations © 'Larry' 1981

This book is set in Linotron 202 Palatino by
Western Printing Services Ltd, Bristol
Printed and bound in Great Britain by
Richard Clay (The Chaucer Press) Bungay, for
J. M. Dent & Sons Ltd
Aldine House, 33 Welbeck Street, London W1

British Library Cataloguing in Publication Data

Briers, Richard
Natter natter.
I. Title
828'.91407   PN6175

ISBN 0-460-04508-3

Contents

1

A Word in Your Ear

I'd better put my cards on the table right from the start and admit that about the only qualification I have for calling myself a conversationalist is a career spent being paid to say other people's lines.

Not that I am ungrateful for this opportunity, quite the reverse. Because I can honestly say that, over the years, one or two of the tricks of the trade have rubbed off on me. And by far the most important thing I've realized is that there's a world of difference between talking and conversation.

Talking is like the mirage that faces the parched man as he staggers through a desert in search of water. Conversation is the oasis that eventually quenches his thirst. As soon as he tastes the water he knows the difference between the real thing and the image. And once he knows it he never forgets.

Let me give you an example of the real thing:

'Ladies and gentlemen,' said Sir Thomas Beecham to one of his audiences, 'In upwards of fifty years of concert-giving before the public, it has seldom been my good fortune to find the programme correctly printed. Tonight is no exception to the rule, and therefore, with your kind permission, we will now play you the piece which you think you have just heard . . .'

Beecham must have drunk from his first oasis very early in life, for in my opinion that display is a wonderful example of conversation. Of course you can argue that technically only Beecham was speaking. But the way he spoke implied that the audience was joining in with him. And what he was saying was witty, succinct, full of good humour and above all supremely effective. There'd been some foul-up with the programme which no one had noticed until the concert had got going and someone had had to put it right, at least that's how I read it. Maybe the orchestra had cheerfully launched into the wrong piece. But whatever the cause of the discrepancy between the programme and the performance, Beecham's command as a conversationalist smoothed things over perfectly.

Few people would deny that Beecham was unique in his conversational ability, and fewer still would deny that such a mastery of the art as his takes years to perfect. But there are some shortcuts, and ingenious ways of helping ourselves out, as I've found from my own line of country, the stage.

And dreary as theory can be (which sounds like a rhyme from Edward Lear) the process of developing our conversation can be considerably helped by following a few simple guidelines.

I keep a marvellous book in the loo at home for moments of contemplation and for longer periods of anguished meditation. In it I've come across a couple of quotes from Ralph Waldo Emerson

which put the art of conversation into a nutshell. The first is the unaffected comment, 'The best in life is conversation.' The second is the somewhat more pointed observation that, 'Conversation is an art in which a man has all mankind for his competitors.' To both of which I say, 'Never were truer words spoken'.

You will probably have noticed that the best conversationalists – say, Robert Morley or Orson Welles – also have fine physiques. According to the experts this is no coincidence. The Victorians regarded conversation as an essentially *athletic* pursuit! One nineteenth-century guru I consulted even insisted that the drawing room conversationalist should have 'a body properly set by gymnastics, fencing, dancing, drill, or other physical exercise'. And so great was his concern for the correct application of this training programme that he even included a footnote stating that: 'A simple and easily accessible means of exercise is the chest expander, made of vulcanized India rubber, a pair of which may be attached to your bedpost, whence they conveniently hang, for daily morning and evening exercise. This is a decided improvement on the old method by dumb-bells, which, however, are better than nothing at all.'

I suppose the general decline in the interest in sport accounts for the absence of such information in modern books about conversation, which is a jolly good thing if, like me, you're not a budding Charles Atlas. About the only advice current manuals do give on the speaker's physical form are a few token remarks about standing erect (though even that phrase is beginning to disappear on the grounds that it's either improper, or sexist) and not putting one's hands in one's pockets. Otherwise the conversationalist is left entirely to his own devices. And should he suddenly collapse with an apoplectic fit in mid-anecdote, seemingly he has only himself to blame. (For collapsing *deliberately* in mid-anecdote, see the section dealing with *Conversation Stoppers*.)

As you will see from the pages that follow I have consulted all the proper authorities, ancient and modern, and I have taken the advice of family, friends and neighbours (those I'm talking to, that is), so my first word is that I hope that *Natter Natter* will be the last word on the subject! I can't guarantee that careful study of the book will turn you into another Oscar Wilde – that probably comes as a relief to some of you – but I do hope it will show you that mastering the art of conversation (or at least trying to!) is one of the most enjoyable aspects of the good life – whatever shape you're in!

2

I Say!

the art of conversation

Attitude – or **Mind Over Chatter**

If you're sitting comfortably, then I'm delighted. The golden rule which I always try to observe when talking to people is to make them feel totally at ease in my company. That's easier said than done.

When I was younger, less experienced in the world and generally rather obnoxious, I was an absolute dead loss at this. I used to suffer terribly from nerves and the result was that I always became very loud and dogmatic, started waving my arms about wildly and eventually came to an embarrassed halt after I'd knocked off someone's specs or tipped half a pint of bitter down their Sunday best.

Middle age has brought more than spread, its brought social mellowness chez Briers. If I want to, I can now make most people feel at ease with me. That's not smugness, it's the hard-earned truth.

All of us have experienced the sort of sinking feeling I used to have before I entered a room full of strangers. And we've all died a thousand deaths on going into the room and the conversation ceases while everyone turns to look at us, and then quickly starts up again, leaving us marooned by the doorway.

In those circumstances I used to be grateful to the bloke who'd shout out, 'Shut the bloody door, will you? It's like the Arctic out there,' because at least it gave me the chance to reply, 'Sorry, I can't just at the moment, there's half Fleet Street just behind me,' or 'I don't think you'd say that if you could see who's just coming,' or 'Hush up mate, I'm keeping an eye on him. Does anyone own a green Ford Zodiac, because it's getting the once-over by the local bobby' – the sort of retort that used to get me into the swing of things.

Even the roughest diamonds can show sympathy to shy strangers and their understanding used to give me the confidence to get stuck into the general drift of the chat. But because they were rough diamonds they didn't flinch from telling me to shut up if I then started to go over the top. 'Put a cake in it, mate,' one of my old chums from Smithfield used to say whenever I got a bit out of hand, and I usually did, though the 'cake' was another half, more often than not.

The sort of sympathetic listener who used to get my back up was the one who would listen to me rabbiting on with a pitying smile that said, 'There, but for the grace of God, go I.' That's an attitude best reserved for those afflicted by halitosis, galloping dandruff and those foolish enough to admit to being VAT inspectors.

I've always found that the simplest way of making someone feel at ease is to draw them into the conversation. If I know something about them beforehand it's easy enough. I just start with that, though, harking back to Beecham for a moment, there's a lesson to be learnt from knowing something, but not quite enough, about the people to whom we speak.

Sir Thomas was returning to his hotel room in Manchester after conducting a concert in the Free Trade Hall. As he entered the foyer he noticed a distinguished-looking woman whom he vaguely recognized, though he couldn't put a name to the face. He realized that she had noticed him, so on the way to the stairs he paused for a few words. In the course of this brief chat he remembered that she had a brother and hoping that this might identify her he asked how her brother was and if he was still in the same job. 'Oh, he is very well,' the lady told him, 'and he is still King.'

12

CONVERSATION STARTERS (No 1)

(If you want to find out how to cope with a crisis like that see the section on *Conversation Stoppers* again, or better still the one on *Emergency Conversation*. They won't make you an instant Beecham, but they won't leave you with egg all over your face, either.)

If I don't know anything about the person to whom I shall be speaking then I usually nab someone in advance who does know him, or her, and get them to give me a thumb-nail sketch. Many's the time I've been grateful for a hastily whispered, '. . . just been banned from driving', or '. . . Henry's ex. She's terribly cut up about it', which have prevented me from setting off on a long account of how I tried to drive through the Dartford Tunnel the wrong way, or the dreadful price of petrol, or the road works on the M.1, or Japanese car sales, on the one hand, and the wonderful family holiday we've just had, or the terrible divorce rate, or how well old Henry's looking after all this time, or asking 'Aren't you the girl we've all been hearing so much about?', on the other.

When I'm absolutely stuck for a starter I tend to plunge in with a topic of my own to test the waters. But unless the elements have suddenly handed one a meteorite, a hurricane or even two consecutive days without rain, on no account should one open up with, 'Lovely weather, isn't it?'. It's just too much of a cliché.

Once I've broken the ice, and there isn't a one hundred per cent success rate by any stretch of the imagination, I try to make the newcomer feel at ease by continuing any existing conversation where I left off. What I've learned not to do is to say things like, 'We must continue this next time,' or 'I'm sure you don't want to be bored with our chatter,' because remarks like these are guaranteed to bring colour to the cheeks of all but the most insensitive intruder.

I reckon that it's just as important not to offend people you're talking to as well, especially if they are in positions of authority. And that can cover anyone from the mother-in-law to traffic wardens.

The purpose of mothers-in-law I can just about accept, but I really don't know what traffic wardens are for, apart from easing the disastrous unemployment situation. However, I'm certain that London, for a start, would be a far easier place to circumnavigate if they did away with traffic wardens and relied on people's common sense.

The trouble with wardens is that you can't reason with them, so any attempt at conversation fails right from the start. Once they've torn out that little piece of paper, that's it.

I honestly believe that they're programmed simply to fine people, so that for whatever reason one is parked on the yellow lines – running to see the wife in a maternity home or going to see an aged relative who's passing away, and we've been five times round the block until in desperation to park we've left the car on a single yellow line, or better still on the pavement – it doesn't worry the traffic warden at all because he, or she, is just there to hand out fines. I do try not to feel too gleeful on wet, windy days when I see one of them stuck outside suffering the torture of the elements.

I decided that traffic wardens were a lost cause after the embarrassment of a friend of mine who tried to pass himself off as a foreigner when he was once booked.

He'd parked on double yellow lines, as we all do from time to time. He was actually only away from the car for a couple of minutes buying an anniversary card for his wife on the way home from work. But when he panted back to his car there was the lady in black and yellow making out her ticket.

'Hi lady,' he said, stretching the use of the noun, but hoping to get off on the right foot by adopting an accent that approximated to that of one of the landmasses in the southern hemisphere, 'What's the problem?'

When she told him that he had parked in the wrong place and was being fined £6 for his pains, he pointed out with nonchalant diplomacy that there was a car parked in front of his, which she hadn't booked. To which the traffic warden replied that its driver was delivering to one of the shops and was therefore exempted.

Now my friend played what he thought was his trump card, 'See here,' he said, 'That car looks pretty much like the one I'm drivin'. How was I to know I couldn't park it here? This isn't even my car, so how about lettin' me off just this once, eh?'

Hearing this, the virago turned on him and said that in those circumstances she could save time and write out the official details there and then, and would he mind telling her the name of his friend whose car he had borrowed, and where he lived.

This threw my chum into an absolute panic. He invented some completely spurious address in Hertfordshire inhabited by one Gordon Dixon, a name hastily contrived from the names of two shops opposite, after being told that he couldn't pay the £6 on the spot.

She asked him a number of awkward questions about Gordon Dixon and he finally left in a bath of perspiration, only to find that he'd left the card on the roof as he'd driven off, and to cap it all he was now twenty minutes late for the most important night of his wife's year.

Over the years I've developed the technique of trying to read what's going on in the mind of the person I'm speaking to. It's one of the best ways of judging how I'm getting on. A look of blank indifference is self-explanatory. An unremitting gaze at some part of my clothing suggests that I should check a few buttons and zips before I get much older.

When I've been a bit out of depth myself, I've developed a strategy of silent interest. It's infinitely preferable to interjecting with the standard repetition of 'Really . . . really . . . really . . . how interesting,' which as one colleague remarked, makes one sound as if one works for the BBC as an interviewer, which in his opinion is the same thing as being a blithering idiot. By following this course I've had time to collect my wits and then seize a suitable opportunity to change the subject. A cow having a pee, a dart sticking into a drinker's neck, a weak gin and tonic have all provided new and diverting topics in their time, allowing me to steer the conversation into less troubled waters before I've opened the bilges and settled them completely with the sludgy oil of a few well-rehearsed pieces.

Approach – or How to Get On

It's never a bad policy to enter a conversation with blind optimism, for approaching it as a form of trial by endurance will make it just that.

Even being lumbered with the greatest bore this side of the Severn can have its rewards. Apart from the virtuous knowledge that, unlike everyone else who has spoken to him, you have avoided being overtly rude (if you have), there is also the double-edged satisfaction that it's almost as worthwhile to have 'one enemy the less' as it is to have 'one friend the more'.

But beware of sticking to the cheerful smile too rigidly. I once found this out to my cost. It's too easy a way out, doesn't require much effort, and I fell into it for that reason. The man I was talking to at the opening night reception was boring beyond words and everyone else had left him as quickly as they could. But Briers wasn't to be put off and as he droned on about the cost-effectiveness of washable nylon and crimplene seat-covers for auditoriums instead of plush velvet, I felt myself slipping into a glassy-eyed stare. So to counteract this a grin spread across my face and stayed.

'I must say it's a refreshing change to meet an actor who appreciates the importance of what goes on in my line of country, as you obviously do, Mr Bowers,' said my friend as he was being led away by his long-suffering wife. 'I'd appreciate your opinion on the range of confectionery on sale in the West End theatres, if you could spare me a few minutes sometime?'

I nodded as he disappeared, silently pleased with my performance in the face of everyone else's undisguised haste to dump the dreadful little man. I may not have got a straight knock-out, but I certainly won on points.

'God, you looked a right Charlie,' said one of the others on the way out. 'If you could have seen yourself standing there, juiced to the gills and grinning like a Cheshire cat, while that little twerp in the dinner jacket held forth nineteen to the dozen. One more gin and you'd have been on the floor, out for the count.'

So, I've given up 'the cheerful smile' as a bad job. It was mistaken so easily for the rigid grin of total intoxication, that people didn't fully appreciate that I was just trying to show good manners. As far as they were concerned, I was more than halfway to passing out.

Only recently have I perfected the right approach for dealing with the painfully shy, probably because until I acquired a bit more confidence, I fell into that category myself. Given a little encouragement, the withdrawn and diffident strangers that I meet on trains, in studios, or anywhere else for that matter often turn out to be delightful company. What I've had to stop myself doing is adopting the 'hail fellow well met' approach of the bluff athlete, who was overheard bellowing into the ear of a pretty wallflower, 'What's your sport, then?' as he battled to make himself heard above the din of the sports club disco.

I remember having a devil of a job once trying to get a word out of a teenage girl I was travelling with in a railway carriage to Leeds. In the end we got onto the subject of demonstrations. There'd recently been a big one in London. Masses of duffle-coated, ragged-haired young people had marched through the streets shouting 'Milk snatcher Thatcher out' (although none of them looked as if they had touched a drop of milk in years). My young companion didn't seem to have much to say on the subject, until I deliberately turned High Tory and muttered, 'I'd throw them all in clink, or cut their grants, that would make them work,' which caught her on the raw. It worked, though, and we had a splendid row for the rest of the journey, extending our discussion into the restaurant car for tea, where we got so heated that neither of us noticed the apologies for sandwiches which BR so kindly offered for sale.

On the whole, I've found that the more humdrum the experience, the greater the chance of drawing out shy companions.

ONE SIDED CONVERSATIONS (No!)

Furtive liaisons with continental waiters are not the daily fare of the majority of the people I meet. But try them on the soaring cost of living, with special reference to the price of cat food in Tesco, or the mediocrity of the tit-bits being sparingly handed round by one's hosts at a party and they will seldom fail to rise to the bait.

Once we've got talking the image of the game comes into play again (so maybe the Victorians weren't so wrong after all) with the ball passing from one speaker to the next. Like all good rugby half-backs though, I never die with the ball if I can help it. If I find that I can't keep the conversation going I desperately try to pass it to someone else before it flounders and has to be rescued from the scrum all over again.

Similarly, if I notice that one of the group is having trouble joining in, I make an effort to side-step the more robust talkers and give the shy one a chance to speak up. This never fails to renew his or her confidence and it's one in the eye for the loudmouths.

However, one of the great paradoxes of conversation is that frequently those who are regarded as the greatest conversationalists are in fact the ones who say the least. Don't be fobbed off by the cynics who tell you that 'No man would listen to you talk if he didn't know that it was his turn next' (Ed Howe). Don't be driven into silence either by the despairing remarks of people like Calvin Coolidge, who once commented, 'If you don't say anything, you won't be called on to repeat it.'

Listening pays tremendous dividends. It was one of the first qualities that I had to master before I could cure my over-animated, red-faced approach which only drove people into their shells. Now, genuinely attentive listening on my part always strikes my companion as a great compliment, even if it is only because I cannot think of anything to say.

There are plenty of boring old maxims that sing the virtues of holding our tongues:

'To listen closely and reply well is the highest perfection we are able to attain in the art of conversation.' (La Rochefoucauld)

'The art of conversation is the art of hearing as well as of being heard.' (Hazlitt)

'It takes a great man to make a good listener.' (Sir Arthur Helps)

But to my way of thinking the greatest advantage of listening is that it helps the listener just as much as it helps the speaker.

There are five reasons why listening is important and useful.

The first is very straightforward. Listening, by its very nature, means that one does not have to speak. And I've always found it an invaluable means of defence in conversations where I've been completely out of my depth.

I once tried to chat with a member of a very *avant-garde* commune that I stumbled across on a holiday in deepest Wales. I soon found that it was quite hopeless. He was happily nattering on about mantras, nirvana and Dharma and all I was hopelessly saying was, 'that must be good karma . . . I bet that gets you up a few more spokes on the wheel of fortune . . . wouldn't fancy coming back as a terrapin myself.' I hadn't the slightest idea what he was going on about. It would have been much better to have shut my mouth and just nodded intelligently once in a while. At least he might have gone off with the idea that I was a potential convert, or even a sage of some sort. But I blew it completely. There's a lesson there.

As well as helping me save face, listening provides valuable time to think of what to say next. This has been terribly useful towards the end of working lunches when I have usually done more lunching than work and taken on board rather more booze than was wise.

Under these circumstances I deliberately moderate my conversation to a few staccato comments muttered with great intensity – 'The Wild Duck . . . eh . . . Vildanden in Norwegian . . . so I believe . . . correct me if I'm wrong . . . No trolls in that of course . . . low on Tolkien-appeal . . .' These sort of things don't actually *mean* anything, they act rather like the preliminaries to, say, a winning putt, or the final serve in the Men's Singles at Wimbledon.

A well-timed pause can be just as unnerving to a companion awaiting your reply as the methodical bouncing of the ball on the back line. And if you let him do all the talking you can martial your thoughts calmly and slowly, listening all the time, except for an occasional, effortless interjection.

In the same way the greatest asset to the traffic policeman in reducing the speeding motorist to a quivering, nervous wreck, is his slow walk back to the offending vehicle. The 'I think we took the last two bends a little hastily didn't we, sir?' is a mere formality compared with the subtle, psychological breakdown of the measured walk to the driver's window and the copper's steely gaze.

Mind you, any motorist worth his salt, or sober enough to stand upright, should ideally call the policeman's bluff in such circumstances, by leaping out of the driver's seat and rushing to the approaching officer waving his arms and screaming, 'You've saved me, you've saved me . . .'. If nothing else, it will throw the officer off his guard. But principally it gives the driver precious moments to think up an excuse.

When I get into a conversation with a person I don't know I always let them do the talking to begin with. This period of listening has saved me many a red face and stammered apology, because it's given me ample time to weigh them up and stopped me from putting my foot in it. Rushing headlong into a conversation has left me open to any number of catastrophes, though none as desperate as that of the unhappy guest at the notorious wedding reception.

Seizing a good-looking stranger by the arm, after noticing his cautious glances at an equally attractive woman, during the wedding speeches, the hostess suggested coyly:

'Do let me introduce you to Marjory. I'm sure you'll have a lot in common. I've only just met her myself, but we got on like a house on fire.'

'Yes, we used to as well,' he told her coldly, 'before we were divorced.'

Reason number four is in many ways the most important. Intelligent listening, punctuated of course by a few pithy remarks, adds emphasis to everything one says, no matter how trivial it may be. I let the others shout their mouths off about the EEC, Welsh language programmes and the three R's, while I merely adopt the all-knowing, all-seeing silence of a Greek chorus. What's more I'm certain that my few contributions are remembered long after all the other claptrap is forgotten.

But as far as I'm concerned reason number five is the crucial one. If you're talking you can't drink. If you listen you can.

Strange as it may sound, sight has proved one of the most useful aids to me when I've been talking. 'Watch the eyes' is as good a maxim to the conversationalist as it is to the tiger-hunter. If they're

closed, it usually means, alas, that my listener has lost interest in what I'm saying. If they're staring fixedly into mine I used to think it was love at first sight, but now I realize that my companion is merely in a state of total panic.

I've learned to be wary, too, of the roving eye which scans the room while I'm talking, with only an occasional glance back at me. This is usually accompanied by a rather languid delivery and a succession of platitudes that require no effort from my companion, who is far more concerned with locating the gin bottle, or keeping out of the way of the bank manager, or looking for someone more interesting to talk to.

If I have to keep a look-out myself, I find it easier to disguise my furtive glances as a nervous tick. This has the added benefit that it tends to encourage my audience either to find less distracting company, or to disappear completely. But this is really a last-ditch measure, for there are certain niceties of conversation which we would do well to observe, and for lack of any better way of describing these I've chosen to include them under etiquette.

Etiquette

The pursuit of etiquette has nowadays become so old-fashioned that it's virtually impossible to draw on modern examples for detailed guidance of etiquette in conversation.

Our great-grandparents were more favourably provided for, though, and as is often the case with Victorian books of self-improvement much of what was written for their instruction makes very amusing reading.

This wonderful extract comes from a work entitled *How to Shine in Society: or the Art of Conversation*, which was written in 1867, a year in which the USA bought Alaska from Russia, in which the Turks withdrew from Belgrade and in which Garibaldi attacked the Papal states in Italy. What it says is good, commonsense stuff, but the language in which it is phrased is uniquely Victorian. In taking its advice we would do well to bear in mind the comment Hamlet's mum made to Polonius about using 'More matter, with less art'!

In general people who have not been introduced are not understood to be on conversing terms. In travelling more freedom is allowed, but even then the conversation is but very general unless special circumstances warrant otherwise.

Who should begin a conversation it is not easy to say. Where there is a doubt as to who should begin, let it be the person of greatest importance in the company. But if it be done modestly any one may begin.

But it is not so difficult to begin a conversation as it is to carry it on successfully. Wit is by no means a sure card. Few can play it well, and still fewer maintain the play. Nor will learning supply you with the material of the right sort altogether. That must pass

through the alembic of your mind and give forth its fine precipitate of thought, and this brings us to the stuff of the proper kind for conversation purposes, for conversation is but the interchange of thought. Learning is dead inert matter that begets nothing, but thought is living spirit and begets thought. It is thought that makes words winged, and hours too.

Look the person in the face with whom you are conversing. Never talk past him – it gives you an air of insincerity. Let your manner be confident without being bold, and easy without being familiar.

Talk neither too slowly nor too quickly, but with a lively degree of raciness. Animation is indispensable to successful conversation. Let the tones of your voice be as musical as possible, steering equally clear of 'clipping' the words of their due amount of sound, or of mouthing them with too much.

25

In general society never alludes to private matters. Talk with the company on subjects of general interest. With learned men you may talk of learned subjects, but never inflict your superior knowledge on people of more slender pretensions. It would be like a rich man displaying his gold against poorer men's copper.

Never interrupt a speaker in what he is saying. If you step before him unceremoniously, it is courteous of him indeed, if he does not take the tempting opportunity of using his foot to take you out of his way.

Never crush any subject of conversation and substitute one of your own in its stead. If you wish it changed, wait till it is exhausted, or lead it in the direction of your own.

Never converse with a pre-occupied mind. Throw your whole mind into it, else you are sure to make the conversation hard and drag 'its weary weight along'.

If unable or not disposed to talk on a subject, you can listen.

It might sound a bit archaic to say so, but most of this seems pretty reasonable to me. Admittedly the point about not alluding to 'private matters' might cramp our style a bit, and deprive many conversationalists of their principal topic, but it would spare the rest of us.

Elsewhere in the book the author makes an important reference to the language that should, or should not, be used in conversation:

Phraseology peculiar to the saloons, clubs, theatres, stables &c. is not allowable on any account, as it is certain to stamp any person who uses it as a 'low fellow'.

The situation today, or so it seems to me, has swung so far in the opposite direction that without the language of the Victorian dens of iniquity mentioned above, we would be left almost speechless.

Even the royal family, in their off-duty moments, are surely not above lapsing into the 'phraseology' of the stables, and certainly the majority of the people who appear on chat shows are there by

virtue of their 'phraseology' peculiar to at least one of the pro-
scribed categories.

The golden rule running through all this advice is surely that
we must *make others feel relaxed and comfortable.*

There are any number of ways of making them feel the *opposite*
when the occasion demands. But the true artist should be able to
rise above this temptation and should look for good points in
everyone with whom he falls into conversation.

When I was a young actor, always on the look-out for roles, the
thing to do was to praise television directors for their work, however bad it might have been. There were precious few good television directors around then, and things aren't much better now –
it's because the poor souls don't get paid very much. But I used to
try to give the impression that I wanted a part in their series
because working with them would greatly improve me as an actor.
A hell of a lot of them saw straight through me, which shows that
etiquette's all very well, but your heart has got to be in what you
say.

I'm ashamed to admit that it took a Frenchman, La Bruyère, to
sum up neatly success in conversation. In his opinion it 'consists
less in being witty than in bringing out the wit in others; the man
who leaves after talking to you, pleased with himself and his wit, is
perfectly pleased with you.'

So much for the theory, then. Now for conversation in practice.

3

Hear Hear!

the craft of conversation

It's always interested me how few people who go into bookshops and libraries, and come out with manuals on D.I.Y., or teach-yourself projects, ever get beyond the sections on theory. So, if you've got this far, don't give up now. No one is going to give a damn whether you can regrind your own crankshaft, speak Albanian, or build a scale-model of Mao's mausoleum from ravioli. But they are going to notice your conversation, or the lack of it.

If we can master conversation, then in the words of the splendid Ethel Cotton, who stood in the vanguard of the socially inept forty years ago, we can win 'Power, Poise and Personality'

'Haven't you always observed that the good conversationalist never lacks poise?' she confided to me when I was in my teens. 'Even with those whom he has never met before, he is instantly at ease. Those who find it hard to be pleasant with others are soon talking to him. No wonder he makes friends everywhere . . . often influential friends who help him advance in the business and social world.

'Very definitely', went on dear Ethel, 'the art of conversation helps give one power. The really good talker has a big advantage in the struggle for success. Where others fail, he forges ahead in all sorts of ways. Think how the art of conversation develops personality. You see abundant evidence of this almost everywhere you go. The man who can talk well . . . there's something about his very presence that makes him welcome in any group! He is so winning in his manner. He greets all he meets in such a friendly way! He is so human . . . so much alive . . . so altogether inspiring. And when he begins to talk, who can help listening! They all want to join in the conversation, and they do!'

The trouble with most of us is that we have a pretty glossy idea of the way we appear to others.

I used to think that I had wonderful presence; that I had limitless charm; that I was amusing, entertaining and engaging in any company. In other words started out in life convinced that dear Ethel had been describing R. Briers Esq. and that I could shake hands with anyone's heart.

Reality, when it dawned, was far from pleasant.

I can remember the first time that I found myself standing outside a door behind which there was neither a single person I knew, nor a single person who would give a damn whether they met me or not. My armpits were saturated. My stomach was heaving. My knees were knocking like castanets. And my hands suddenly felt three times their normal size and had nowhere to go. All my polished lines flew out of my head and when I opened my mouth to greet my hostess all that came out was a string of falsetto barks, followed by a helpless fit of coughing.

After that brush with reality I started to take a bit more interest in how other people managed to get on so well and the first thing I noticed was that I'd got off on the wrong foot right from the start, simply because I'd made no effort to prepare myself properly.

So my first task on the road to recovery was learning how to open a conversation.

The Beginning

If, unlike me, you're blessed with the gift of the gab, then this section is not for you. If you're not then read on. (At least you're honest with yourself.)

Once I'd started to take an interest in what others were saying it

struck me that effortless and natural as the good conversationalists' opening gambits appeared to be, they were the products of as
much care and practice as the best speeches of a Churchill or a
Hoffnung.

I also noticed that they had a store of amusing little gems
which they had gleaned from the gossip columns or from eaves-
dropping on the conversations of celebrities. So I began to collect
these gobbits myself.

I read the sports pages of the quality newspapers and even
acquired a passing interest in racing as a side-line. I made a point of
reading the Court Circular because the Royal Family go down well
everywhere. You can drop them into a conversation with Willie
Hamilton just as easily as you can if you are hobnobbing with
the Duke of Norfolk. And in view of the fact that Her Majesty once

graced us to watch the recording of a programme of *The Good Life* I now quite legitimately pepper my conversational openings with remarks like, 'When I was last talking to Her Majesty,' or 'As the Queen last said to me . . .', or 'Knowing the Royal Family as I do . . .', which sound splendid and get me off to a flying start all round.

This helps me to give the impression that I regularly bump into leading world figures, but I stop short of adopting the manner of most of the journalists I meet, who make no bones of the fact that they could solve all the world's problems, but no one has offered them enough money to do so yet.

One of the few social blessings of being an actor is that it does equip one for learning these bits of introductory material, which come in so handy for filling in those dreadful pauses after you've been introduced and in which your mind goes a complete blank.

What I tend to do now is to jump in with a complete non-sequitur immediately I feel a pause coming on. I've got a stock pile of bizarre information and fascinating biographical oddities about the great, the not so great and the downright obscure, which usually see me through:

'I've always wondered how they knew that Jack the Ripper was left-handed? You don't have any idea I suppose? Or are you left-handed and frightened to say?'

'Have one of these. The Aztecs thought they were aphrodisiacs but they only gave me spots and tummy ache.' (This one's quite useful because it can include anything from chocolates to guinea pigs).

'I see you've met Tony's mother-in-law. The Lhopa tribe in Tibet celebrate a marriage by eating the bride's mother, you know.'

'What's the difference between a duck? You don't know? Well, one of its legs is both the same.'

. . .

These are the kind of bald, terse statements that seldom fail to elicit a response, even if it's just a startled request to repeat what you said. But even that starts the ball rolling.

If your memory is a bit dodgy, however, there's nothing wrong with sharing a few personal experiences, which are always good for a laugh. And the people I warm to the quickest are the ones who make me laugh.

I was once standing next to an unprepossessing-looking man as we queued to pay for our pre-Budget booze in the supermarket:

'I don't know about you,' he suddenly said, 'but I have a dickens of a job getting out of that new car park they've built next to this place. The last time I tried to feed money into the damned machine at the exit, it chewed up my ticket, gave me two quid in assorted change and then smashed the barrier down on the roof of the Mini that was coming through after me.'

This story quickly broke the ice (although I expect the bonhomie of getting one up on Denis Healey also eased the atmosphere), and soon all the people in the queue were joining in with their respective views on the local planning department and why a municipal sports centre would have been so much more worthwhile. A second disastrous story soon came from a man clasping eight bottles of Haig without the slightest appearance of feeling self-conscious:

'Well, that's nothing,' he confided to us, 'My wife, Ethel and I went to Blackpool last summer and Ethel got trapped in the lift at the top of the Tower. They couldn't get the fire engine inside to let her out either and if it hadn't been for a busker with a performing monkey she might still be there.'

A similar narrow escape story was told to me by a man sitting in the gardens of Hampton Court as we watched one of the gardeners cutting the lawn.

'It is the thirteenth today, isn't it?' he said. 'The reason I ask is that I nearly came a cropper this time last year. Damned silly really. I didn't think at the time, but it gave me a hell of a shock I can tell you. I got rid of the blasted thing straight away, so I can still cut the lawn in bare feet. But it never occurred to me that the damp grass could give one an electric shock. I'd just stepped onto the crazy paving to turn round, when the lead got snagged on a rose bush and got tied up with the blade. It didn't do the gladioli much good, 240 volts through their stakes. But it could have been the chop for me if I hadn't been on terra firma, so to speak. You got a mowing machine, have you?'

An equally effective way of making your companion feel at home early on in your conversation is to share secrets with him, or her. They don't have to be risqué, or even libellous. The fact that a stranger has chosen to confide in you is reward enough.

We were asked round to a house-warming party a few years ago by a very strange couple who had a thing against flowers and a penchant for rockeries, which meant that we had to step through what looked like the aftermath of the Blitz to get to the front-door. We didn't know a soul there and were on the point of drinking up and making a run for it when an elderly lady sidled up to us and whispered:

'They'll kill me if they find out I've let on. But it's all home-made, every drop. Even the Pernod, though God knows how they did it. There's not a flower in the garden, and if you ask me they've mushed up the whole lot to make the drinks. Have you ever seen sherry this colour before?'

And she lifted a glass of grey-coloured liquid to the light of the naked electric bulb.

The odd couple only lasted a few months, no doubt because the flowers refused to stop growing. But we got quite chummy with the sherry lady.

There are a couple of old favourites for breaking the ice, which are as old as the hills, but which, like the hills, still have their attractions, if they're approached from a new direction.

Holidays that we've had, are about to have, would have had if it hadn't been for the au pair eloping with the vicar, or are planning for our retirement, are old stand-bys, but they can still be of interest provided they include a few unusual details, or include travel to interesting places. (Incidentally, Torquay and Clee-thorpes have recently been reintroduced into this category.)

Accounts must be brief and phrased in a manner which will immediately engage the attention of one's companion. There's no earthly point in trying to captivate an audience if all one can offer them is a rain-soaked fortnight in Frinton – unless your hotel burned to the ground or you found yourself sitting at the next table to Kevin Keegan.

I've found that it's best not to go into raptures about Samarkand or Bali either, at least not until I've sounded out my companions to check that firstly they know where they are, and secondly that they have some interest in oriental travel.

By far the safest bet is to offer a racy anecdote of how you shared a bridal suite with half-a-dozen models promoting Kleenex. Any men listening will be green with envy and in some cases the story will remind them of double bookings that they had on their own holidays, which might then lend you some credibility.

My final resort is to fall back on the family. Most parents can talk for hours about their children, but when faced with any other subject scarcely a word will pass their lips.

You've got to watch how you introduce the subject, though. Don't, whatever you do, try to get going with remarks like, 'I expect yours are well beyond school age,' or, 'You were so lucky not to have to cope with this new Maths,' which I've come out with before now. It's always far safer to go for a more general question like, 'How did you decide on where to educate yours?' because this leaves open the question as to what stage in their education the children have reached, and by implication how old the parents are.

It's always struck me as being safer, too, not to enquire directly about what people do for a living. Experience has taught me that this information will be volunteered by the successful and will be glossed over by the failures.

There's absolutely no need to wade in with both feet as a doctor chum of mine did when he asked the wife of the hospital's previous catering manager why her old man had been sacked. He knew perfectly well that they'd somehow managed to buy a house in Spain, which struck everyone as being a bit odd at the time, since the bloke barely earned enough to keep him above the bread-line. If my friend had only stopped to think for a minute he would have put the pad in Spain and the marked deterioration in the canteen food together and come up with the answer for himself. It's all a case of forethought.

A much simpler way of finding out about someone you've just met is to discover what they do in their spare time.

I've boiled every conceivable human activity down to seven broad topics: art, dramatic performances, literature, music, politics, social activities and sports.

Under *art* I group personal participation in anything from water-colours to tattooing, as well as lectures, visits to galleries and coffee-table books sent by book clubs.

I let *dramatic performances* cover theatre, cinema, television, radio plays, street theatre and amateur theatre (in that order).

Literature is fairly obvious. It covers reading, subscribing to book clubs, buying the TLS and writing for pleasure on paper, lavatory walls and in the margins of library books.

In recent years *music* has become less easy to define. I feel fairly safe with the classics, opera and ballet. Jazz, the Beatles and Mantovani, and sometimes folk singing, fall into this category, too. But the wilder excesses of punk rock leave me completely at sea and I've never ventured to explore them.

People you meet at parties and other social do's who immediately collar you and fill you with politics shouldn't have been invited in the first place and should certainly be ditched as soon as possible. I find discussing the subject in public odious enough, but anyone who openly admits to spending his free time following the goings-on in the political world goes down in my book as a social leper right away.

On the other hand, like a bee shot up with pollen, I beam in on those who like having a good time, and know a good *social activity* when they see one. People like this are usually worth being cultivated in the hope of a future invitation. Barbecues, whist drives, assignations in restaurants, pubs, discos and bingo may not be the hallmarks of the most cultivated man, but they might indicate better company than the bore who offers us a three-quarter-of-an-hour summary of the Income Tax changes in the last budget and how he's worked them to his advantage yet again, in spite of what the Chancellor was trying to do.

Even though I'm not much of an athlete myself, *sports* are still a pretty safe bet. Even if I find I'm talking to someone who doesn't look as if he's moved faster than a pedigree tortoise for the last fifty years, he will probably have some comment to make on those who have. And with the added dimension of the Olympic boycott, sports can now encompass moral and ethical issues on a far wider scale than the ones raised by the sight of armies of middle-aged women leering at all-in wrestling matches.

Naturally trying to draw someone out on their pet topic runs the risk of losing control of the conversation, but it does give me a chance of discovering what makes him tick and helps me decide how to carry on our chat.

And all this is terribly important for anyone who wants to be classified as Good Company.

In fact a look back to the advice dished out to our great-grandparents shows that they employed similar strategies. In 1891 the author of *Conversational Openings: Some hints for the game of small talk* gave some splendid words of advice. (The book itself was part of an equally splendid series that rejoiced in the name of *The Dullard's Handbook Series*.) Here's what he said in the introduction:

'All I wish to do is to suggest a few formulas which may prove useful to the dull – a series of Conversational Openings, so to speak, in the sense of Chess openings, the acquirement of which will lead insensibly to mastering the next step.'

And in following his 'dream', '. . . to hide the joins of life, as it were, to fill up some of the unsightly gaps of existence', he offers this gem of advice: 'One platitude at the right moment is worth a dozen repartees the next morning.'

The examples which follow are drawn from a world which has long since disappeared. But in their grace and delicacy, they are models which we would lose nothing in following.

These are my favourites:

At table

If the players are unequally matched:

Black (Man)	White (Lady)
(1) Do you say drink soup, or eat soup?	(1) I really don't know – I don't think I say either.
(2) What do you say, then?	(2) I really don't know – I don't think I say anything.

If the players are well matched:

Black (Man)	White (Lady)
(1) Do you say eat soup, or drink soup?	(1) That is a question I have spent my life trying to solve.
(2) You may not say to 'take' it either, I believe.	(2) No, certainly not! It is a most difficult problem, etc.

This is a promising beginning, and should within six or seven remarks lead to a discussion on the influence of contemporary fashion on the transformation of the language.

Temperance Opening

Black (Man)	White (Lady)
(1) Might I ask you to pass me the water?	(1) Certainly. Are you a teetotaller?

In four moves Man should now be in the middle of the discussion on temperance.

Geographical Opening

This will succeed where almost every other fails and besides it can be combined with the well-worn Weather Opening, e.g.:

Black (Man)
(1) How wretched the weather has been!

(2) Really! Are you a cockney?

White (Lady)
(1) Yes, indeed, though I ought to be accustomed to the weather in London, as it is my native air.

Aunt's Friend's Opening

White (Lady)
(1) I think you know my aunt.
(2) Yes, Mrs Mackay.

Black (Man)
(1) Your aunt?
(2) Oh, to be sure, yes – we met in the Engadine last year.

This can always be combined with the Geographical opening.

After Dinner Opening

Black (Man)
(1) We have been having a most interesting discussion since you left us.

White (Lady)
(1) Indeed. What about?

This, of course, assumes that Black has some foundation for his assertion. It would not do to begin thus:

Black (Man)
(1) I have eaten a whole of a dish of almonds and raisins since we parted.

So much for the guidelines of ninety years ago.

Once I started to feel my way in conversation I became a bit more daring and began to look around for ways to keep the chat flowing, as well as ways of preventing myself from becoming hopelessly lost, or bored to distraction by others.

These are some of the tactics that I picked up on the way.

The Next Step

Most manuals on conversation advise the reader to start compiling a note-book. I started to do so and found it invaluable. Some of what I jotted down appears later, but I can strongly recommend the practice to anyone interested in never being at a loss for anything to say.

I tried to make a point of noting down something every day. Bon mots, pithy aphorisms, amusing anecdotes, jargon, or simply neat ways of expressing the commonplace all found their way into my little book. The process certainly reaped its rewards. My memory started to improve and I became far more attentive to what was going on around me.

Really dedicated types use their note-books for personal debriefing after every conversation. I've always felt this was a bit too self-conscious. Besides I never have the courage to be that honest with myself. I don't really mind too much what other people think of my conversation but I loathe picking holes in it myself the morning after the night before.

I use my little book as an annexe of my memory. It used to live reassuringly in my pocket, but now it shares a schizophrenic existence between the bedside table and the loo.

Being a fairly simple soul, I was always quite content to let the conversation bounce from one speaker to another, with me in the middle giving it a little uplift once in a while, with one of my little gems. Things would be fine until someone showed signs of monopolizing the conversation, by which I mean not letting me get a word in edgeways. This used to make me hot under the collar and it was only the greatest self-control that prevented me from resorting to the youthful expediency of waving my arms about and getting red in the face.

41

In the end I stumbled on the secret which had been staring me in the face all along – change the subject, but without making it too obvious. Statements like, 'Quite so. But if I might be allowed to continue where I left off . . .' only caused antagonism because they were boorish and clumsy. Subtle nudges towards another topic, however, became a clever form of verbal judo. They turned the other speaker's momentum against himself.

The simplest way of doing this is slyly to introduce a new subject associated with the one under discussion, but which can be used to steer the conversation gradually in the direction in which one wants it to go. It is really a straightforward association of the ideas game.

I got into a heated argument once about the fate of the country-side. There were really two main participants with me in the middle acting as a sort of referee. The older of the two was a diehard, Tory landowner who refused to be diverted from firing broadsides at the local planning authority. After a while the other chap, who started off as being by far the milder of the two, began to introduce the subject of environmental protection.

This was like a red rag to a bull. The older man started holding forth against 'busy-body, do-gooding legislation,' and, 'so-called experts with woven ties and beards, who don't even know the difference between landscaping and developing.' This was just what the other chap wanted and he gently led the conversation along the path of 'preserving the national heritage' before mounting his own hobbyhorse and embarking on an equally heated account of Dutch Elm Disease and its effects on undertakers, who, he claimed, would have run out of coffin boards in five years' time.

The big snag with most such bores is that they refuse to be diverted from their pet topic (though how many of us would freely give it up?). The solution I came to was to halt the idiot in mid-sentence by asking his advice about something.

This is about the only effective way I've come across for dealing, too, with back-bores, heart-bores, psychological bores and all the other hypochondriacs who ramble on, given half a chance.

BRAVE REPLIES (No!)

But I must confess to falling into this category myself when there's no one around, like my wife, to stop me. Some years ago I had a condition known as parathyroid which could only be cured apparently by cutting my throat from ear to ear. As a result, I have a wonderful reason for monopolizing any vaguely medical conversation by posing as a contemporary Ben Gunn and holding my chin up to see if people can find the scar.

So, the sort of interruptions which I tried to make were interesting ones like this:

'I'm sorry to cut across you, but I was fascinated by what you were saying about the corset with the zip that ran from your knees to your neck. Do you think it would be any good for the gardener? The poor old boy's suffered with sciatica for years and now he can't even bend down to pick the strawberries.'

Without a doubt, however, the safest way of diverting any conversation must be the sudden-interest technique. A new view, some bizarre object of interest, a brilliant shop display, a streaker – all provide an ideal excuse for cutting in with a comment like,

43

'Sorry to stop you in full flight, Harry, but you shouldn't miss that blonde on the bicycle . . . the one with the yellow trousers. You know the type, shoe horn to get into them, potato peeler to get out. Over there looking in the window of the butcher's . . .'

The only thing to watch is that what you're about to point out is really what you intend it to be. So often desperation builds up to the point that almost anything will do. The golden rule is to look before you leap.

It's sheer suicide to adopt the policy of the bored guest who was fed up with listening to his host droning on about the problems of matching metric and imperial tile sizes and suddenly shouted, 'Hey look out of the window,' without checking first. Everyone turned round and saw a couple of dogs locked in mutual enjoyment. The guest never got invited again. The other major point which I've had drummed into me about changing the subject of a conversation is that it really ought to be done for the benefit of everyone else in earshot. People who change conversation solely to exercise their own tongues are easily seen through, and they rapidly become as loathsome as the bores they are trying desperately to divert.

In fact I've been trained now not to stifle a bore unless I know that what I'm going to say is of greater interest and appeal.

What really makes for dull listening is the loosely-woven, theoretical argument which says in a quarter of an hour what one well-judged example says in a quarter of a minute. One concrete example of a seventy-two hour wait in the departure lounge at Luton is worth twenty minutes invective against Spanish air-traffic-controllers. So I always try to be positive and give my audience something to get their teeth into.

Some actors are particularly tedious and long-winded. It's usually a sign that they're struggling, and interestingly it usually happens when they're talking to other actors about the theatre.

Now I've always taken a very great interest in the theatre of the past and I find that very few actors know anything about the history of their profession, and this is usually borne out by the sort of woolly nonsense that they come out with when they are talking about the great names of the past. So the way that I cut in and change the subject is to shoot out lines like, 'Of course you need the charm of a Hawtrey,' or, 'The trouble about him is that he needs the speed of a Ralph Lynn and the presence of a Kean.' (It's not unknown either for someone to ask me, '. . . the presence of a keen what?')

One of the few points in which fate has given me a head start in conversation is the sort of animated, agreeable warm humanity which everyone expects me to exude.

Let's face it, most of us spend a good deal of our time locked in conversation with one person at the village fête or over the mulled wine after the annual carol singing, when we would far rather be chatting to the blonde running the tombola, or even the blonde collecting the hymn books. But if we remember the silvery lining to every cloud, it's just possible that the senile old fool who's telling us his life story, and has just got to the General Strike, might be the young lady's favourite grandparent.

She knows that, 'he does go on a little . . .', but 'he's an absolute darling, really.' And far more importantly she knows that, 'It was terribly sweet of you to spend so much time listening to him,' and, 'You and I are going to get on very well together.'

So, here are one or two tips which help me conceal my fatigue and indifference and give the impression that I'm having a wonderful time listening to them and occasionally saying something very important or clever myself.

Repartee

Repartee is the gift with which all the great conversationalists seem to be born and which the rest of us bring into play the morning after the night before, while we're staring bleary-eyed into the bathroom mirror, trying to see how we could have come out better from last night's row in the pub about the juke-box.

Repartee is the ready reply, the quick retort, and the sparkling wit which raises Oscar Wilde and his like head and shoulders above the rest of us.

Here are a couple of examples from two of them, Thomas Moore from the eighteenth century and G. K. Chesterton from our own:

> **Moore's father**: 'Come, come, at your time of life, there's no longer excuse for thus playing the rake. It is time you should think, boy, of taking a wife.'
> **Moore**: 'Why, so it is, father – whose wife shall I take.'

> **Young woman**: (handing out feathers to men not in uniform in 1915) to Chesterton: 'Why aren't you at the front?'
> **Chesterton**: 'Young lady, if you will come round to my side you will see that I am.'

Repartee also makes use of associations of ideas, which can either be absurd and therefore funny, or which can function like in this one:

'He's such a perfect host. You can see that he always makes his guests feel at home.'

'Yes – even when he wishes they were.'

Repartee is jolly useful, too, for making people look absolute fools. Again it's a sort of intellectual judo which most great brains have indulged in at some time or another – even Milton.

He'd got into rather hot water after the Restoration of Charles II, because during Cromwell's effort at being king in all but name, Milton had made little effort to hide his anti-royalist sympathies. He'd even been rash enough to write in support of Charles I's execution, which wasn't guaranteed to endear him to the new king.

In fact when they met, Charles couldn't refrain from suggesting to the blind poet that his handicap might be heavenly retribution for trying to muck about with the divine right of kings.

'Sir,' replied Milton, 'It is true that I have lost my eyesight. But if all calamitous providences are to be considered as divine judge-

ments, your majesty should remember that your father lost his
head.'

That taught the Merry Monarch to hold his tongue.

I quickly learned, though, that it's a mistake to base all my
repartee on original, Briers, off-the-cuff remarks – there aren't
enough of them to go around. Many's the time when I've been in a
desperate need of something pithy to say and my creative powers
have been on short time. But there's always been a second line of
defence which comes easy to an actor, and that's to use someone
else's instead. As long as you give the source of your remark, this is
perfectly acceptable.

47

What's even better, though, is to come out with an anonymous aphorism. If it's recognized, no one can accuse you of plagiarism. If it isn't, it sounds good anyway. (Should any pedantic fool ask you where your bon mot comes from, just say nonchalantly, 'Chinese proverb, my own translation.' That will shut him up.)

Actually Chinese proverbs do make rather good aphorisms anyway, providing you can find one to fit the bill:

'To know what we know, and know what we do not know, that is wisdom.'

'It is better to grow a branch than cut off a limb.'

'A gentleman considers what is right; the small man considers what will pay.'

Such remarks add tone and weight to any conversation. But they've got to be used sparingly, like garlic. If we season our conversation with a string of aphorisms like these, we'll only end up like Polonius – stabbed behind an arras. But if you are willing to risk the occasional flash of blinding aphoristic brilliance here are some gems to choose from:

'Life is one long process of getting tired.' (Samuel Butler)

'Every woman should marry – and no man.' (Benjamin Disraeli)

'The object of art is to give life a shape.' (Jean Anouilh)

'Middle age is when wherever you go on holiday you pack a sweater.' (Denis Norden)

'Most people would die sooner than think: in fact they do so.' (Bertrand Russell)

'Ashes to ashes and clay to clay; if the enemy don't get you, your own folk may.' (James Thurber)

'It seldom pays to be rude. It never pays to be only half rude.' (Norman Douglas)

'The art of acting consists of keeping people from coughing.' (Sir Ralph Richardson)

'Asking a working writer what he thinks about critics is like asking a lamp-post how it feels about dogs.' (Christopher Hampton)

'An actor's a guy who, if you ain't talking about him, ain't listening.' (Marlon Brando)

I can't deny, though, that I'm probably more suited to the fool's coxcomb than the scholar's cap. But then we all harbour our private illusions. And humour does help to reduce life's problems to a manageable size. It pours oil on the rusty machinery of getting along with others. It helps us see the ridiculous as it really is. And it provides a convenient line of escape from those conversations which start to turn rather sour. Besides, most of us have a sense of humour of some sort or another. It may not be the most polished, but it's a start.

This is where the note-book comes in handy, too. It doesn't take much practice to note down something funny everyday. The newspapers alone offer plenty of scope, if only from their misprints or their ambiguous headlines. Recording these may not turn us into a Groucho Marx overnight but they will save us from being branded as totally humourless.

And of course the natural follow-on to developing a reservoir of humorous material, is the art of telling a good story.

Anecdotes

Unlike a lot of other conversational material which I've collected, anecdotes can, and often do, form conversational centre-pieces in their own right.

Having said which, I am reminded of Agnes Repplier's timely warning in her 1904 essay *The Luxury of Conversation* which she in turn takes from Thomas De Quincey:

49

'Of all the bores whom man in his folly hesitates to hang, and Heaven in its mysterious wisdom suffers to propagate his species, the most insufferable is the teller of good stories.'

To which she adds the comment:

'This is a hard saying. The story, like its second cousin the lie, has a sphere of usefulness. It is a help in moments of emergency, and its serves admirably to illustrate a text. But it is not, and never can be, a substitute for conversation.'

Which I absolutely agree with, even if it does make things a bit more difficult for us.

Stories told in the middle of conversation should always link up with what is being said. Whenever they fail to do so, they just become a series of unrelated recollections and jokes, each trying to outrun the other and none of them getting anywhere.

The type of humorist I try to avoid like the plague is the one who joins a conversation simply to come out with the latest story he's picked up, irrespective of whether it has any bearing on what is being talked about or not.

We got landed with one of these oafs on holiday once (it's curious how one's fellow countrymen always seem so much worse when they're abroad). There'd been some rumours about counterfeit currency drifting about the hotel and as it was in the days when the British were allowed to take only £25 out of the country, this was a topic of not inconsiderable interest to those of us who used to spend half the meal doing sums on the back of the table cloth to see if we could afford another half-litre of local wallop.

Anyhow, this cheerful Charlie joined our financial debate, caught the drift of what we were saying and then came out with, 'You know that reminds me of a story I was once told . . .'

Of course we didn't know, so we let him carry on.

'There was this old girl, loaded with all that money could buy, who had a pretty jumped-up idea of her skill on the piano,' he informed us, beaming with success already. 'One day she invited all the toffs round to her place for a recital in which she was going to star. When the time came for her to do her party piece, she got some poor young beggar to turn the pages for her as she played. Her playing was so awful, though, that when she finished she thought she'd better say something to him. So she whispered, 'I hope the false note wasn't too obvious.' To which this young bloke said, 'Which one?'

'What's that got to do with what we were talking about before?' asked one of the others.

'Well . . . false notes, counterfeit money . . . it's a sort of pun,' he informed us blithely. 'You know, a play on words.'

'Oh,' replied our spokesman, and the quorum broke up without any decision on the money issue.

Like the examination candidate who, I always think, is well advised to have three facts, two jokes and a conclusion for every topic, the best conversationalists seem to have, in the words of Robert Louis Stevenson, '. . . a fact, a thought, an illustration pat to every subject.' These they pick up from other people as much as from newspapers or books, and you and I pick them up from them.

Here are a few of the ones that have gone into the Briers

collection over the years, with the headings under which I attempt to classify them:

Mothers-in-law (for some reason, always a fruitful topic for conversation).
The famous Irish peer and lawyer Lord Russell of Killowen was once asked by a distinguished barrister what the severest penalty was for bigamy. Without a moment's hesitation he answered, 'Two mothers-in-law.'

Sam Goldwyn (apparently the originator of remarks like 'A verbal contract isn't worth the paper it's signed on,' 'A bachelor's life is no life for a single man,' and 'Include me out.').
Goldwyn decided that with the wide sale of the notorious (at the time) *The Well of Loneliness* he might make a bid for the film rights.
    'You can't make a film about that,' one of his lawyers told him 'It's all about Lesbians.'
    'OK,' replied Goldwyn, 'I'll use Austrians instead.'

Authors The great actor-manager, Sir Herbert Beerbohm Tree (one of the 'greats' in the Briers canon) wrote this masterly reply to a dramatist who'd asked for some advice on his latest attempt, 'My dear sir, I have read your play. Oh my dear Sir! Yours faithfully, Tree.'

Diplomacy Sir Anthony Eden was once asked by a reporter what effect Stalin's death would have on international affairs. 'That's a good question for you to ask,' Eden told him, 'And not a wise one for me to answer.'

Marxisms 'No, Groucho is not my real name. I'm breaking it in for someone else.'

    'Excuse me, Mr Marx,' an Italian priest said to Groucho, 'my mother was a great fan of yours.'

'I didn't know you guys were allowed to have mothers,' Groucho told him.

William Cowper wrote a long poem on *Conversation* two centuries ago. Two couplets from this sum up all we need to remember about anecdotes in our conversation:

> A tale should be judicious, clear, succinct,
> The language plain, the incidents well linked;
> Tell not as new what everybody knows,
> And, new or old, still hasten to a close.

How to Create the Right Impression

The sum of all the previous hints really boils down to creating the right impression. This includes making others feel at ease, showing interest in what they have to say, making sure that everyone has a chance to put in a word, and not dominating the conversation ourselves. All this is fairly straightforward.

There are other occasions, however, when we find ourselves completely at sea, and these call for special tactics. I have to force myself not to back down from such encounters and to look at them as challenges. It doesn't come as much of a consolation either to think that the person I'm talking to is probably having just as much trouble weighing me up and deciding how to cope.

I don't know about you, but I find it unnerving that confrontations like this always seem to happen with influential people. Even if I'm trying to talk about something which doesn't concern me directly, I always break into a sweat at the thought that what I say and do might make a difference to someone else, especially the family. So I get into a real flap trying not to appear a complete ignoramus, which doesn't help at all.

School teachers have always been rather a vexed question to me, because they're like doctors, starting in a one-up position.

It's really just memories of the beaks from my own schooldays that put me on edge when we go along to the Parent-Teachers meetings, but these are still some of the worst evenings in my year. Queuing to chat to each member of staff for twenty minutes puts me into a one-down position right away.

I try to exchange a few words with the other parents, but it's usually no use. I feel as if I'm on the carpet myself, and when I rack my brain trying to work out what Lucy, or Katy said about her performance in Biology or Maths, I'm suddenly haunted by memories of my own school reports. The result is that by the time I sit down to chat to the French mistress (whose name I can never remember, except for the one the kids call her) I'm fiddling with my handkerchief and completely tongue-tied.

'You're Lucy Briers's father, of course,' she says.

'Yes, sir,' I answer immediately.

'Well, we were quite pleased with the exam result this term. I think you'll agree that's an improvement on the last time?'

'Thank you,' I say, grinning sheepishly.

'But there's still this old block with irregular verbs which we really must try to overcome before the start of the 'O'-level work.'

'Yes,' I reply vaguely, because quite honestly I could pass a French verb in the street tomorrow without recognizing it, let alone know whether it was regular or not.

'And we all think that you could help here by testing at home and maybe lending the odd helping hand now and again to give just that little bit of extra encouragement.'

This of course is what I've been dreading all evening. If anyone needs a helping hand with their French irregularities it's R. Briers. I'm a pastmaster at giving the *entente cordiale* more than a generous shot of angostura bitters. But you can't let the kids down in the face of the powers-that-be, so I agree lamely and make a note to write off to those people on the back page of the daily paper who claim to turn you into a polyglot in eighteen easy lessons. (They never work with me. But I enjoy the music at the beginning, and the English voices are always a scream.) As far as the kids are concerned, though, it means another Easter trip to France and more evenings listening to Edith Piaf and Françoise Hardy.

The worst thing one can do is to be too specific in what one says under these circumstances. Nothing gives us away as much as committing ourselves too freely to what we think is right.

I've had to guard against seemingly innocent questions like, 'How many violin concertos was it that Beethoven wrote?' (to the music mistress) and 'Rachel Heyhoe-Flint, marvellous horse-woman' (to the games mistress).

When I'm faced with other company I reckon I come out slightly better, because I'm not afraid to stand my ground. And here I've grown to appreciate the value of never admitting my ignorance.

Vague, yet plausible detractions have seen me through several scrapes when I could easily have made a fool of myself, but have managed to come out instead with the reputation of being a slightly unbending, but nevertheless firm critic of anything from formula one cars to the musical outpourings of a lesser-known disciple of Stockhausen.

In my ignorance I've been known to comment of Kandinsky that he 'dipped his brush in shade'. Of a concert performance by a leading, young Finnish pianist that I accidentally claimed to have attended, I simply remarked darkly, 'very heavy-fingering I'm afraid'. In fact my policy in dealing with the arts is aptly summed up by Byron who wrote, 'Not to admire is all the art I know.'

This actually links up with what I was saying earlier about the importance of being a good listener. Long pauses and long words certainly help to spread out my scanty knowledge.

As I mention later I use jargon words to give what I say a veneer of acceptability as well. This is a marvellous way of getting off on the right foot and it stops the inquisitive from probing too deeply into my knowledge. Inevitably, however, this is really only a rear-guard action and sooner or later one's luck runs out and one finds oneself with one's back to the wall.

But even this needn't be hopeless, as countless political speeches and the testimonies of hardened criminals have shown us. A famous reply given by Richard Nixon's press secretary, which probably spans both these categories, shows exactly how to deal with what the rest of us would regard as the final straw. Asked by a group of reporters during the Watergate exposure whether a batch of the tapes were still intact, instead of answering 'yes' or 'no', Ronald Ziegler told them:

> I would feel that most of the conversations that took place in those areas of the White House that did have the recording system would in almost their entirety be in existence but the special prosecutor, the court, and, I think the American people are sufficiently familiar with recording systems to know where the recording devices existed and to know the situation in terms of the

recording process but I feel, although the process has not been undertaken yet in preparation of the material to abide by the court's decision, really, what the answer to that question is.

If you can come up with answers like that, you probably know all there is to know about the craft of conversation.

4

Oops!

conversations of a delicate nature

I reckon that one of the greatest compensations of being middle-aged is that you stop being embarrassed by things which used to turn you puce at an early age. I was always frightfully shy and this led to me being embarrassing in the worst possible way. I used to speak very fast and loud, and to make matters worse I made wild gesticulations, like a sort of juvenile Magnus Pyke.

Mercifully those days have gone. Today I can spill soup down my front, knock over a pyramid of baked bean tins in Sainsburys and approach any potentially awkward situation without so much as a raised word or a flick of the wrist. But it wasn't so long ago that any conversation of a delicate nature filled me with trepidation and gave the palms of my hands a nasty, clammy feeling.

My nerves used to bring on an aggressive turn in my manner that always achieved exactly the opposite effect to the one I wanted. Instead of easing the situation with my own polished confidence, I almost invariably put other people's backs up and came out of the encounter ruffled, not to say fleeing with my tail between my legs.

Well can I sympathize with the well-meaning blunderer who approached a fellow-passenger on the platform at Euston with:

'Pardon me, but . . . um . . .'

only to be spurned with:

'No, you've never met me at Biarritz, Cannes or Bognor. I never travel on the Central Line at 8.45. I know that I'm good looking and that I remind you of your sister. I'm not getting off at your station and I wouldn't accept a lift from you if you owned the only car in England. I didn't go to school with you. I'm not waiting for a bus. It's not about to rain and my boy friend is in the SAS. Now, were you about to say something?'

'Yes, damn it, your knickers are falling down.'

Whenever possible, conversations of a delicate nature should not be handled like this. The tactful commuter would have done much better to come straight out with a jolly line like, 'Hey, love, you're losing your drawers', or something like that. Where he, I and, I suspect, most of the male population of this country come a cropper is in the momentary hesitation when our nerve fails. What middle age teaches is how to be prepared at moments like this.

We would all dearly love the practised ease of the smoothy who can come out with lines like this: 'Delightful as all these suggestions sound, I'm afraid that my intentions were far more mundane. As they say in gentlemen's lavatories, kindly adjust your dress.'

This sort of reply is marvellous. It is brief. It says exactly what it is meant to say, and it has the other great merit of giving the silly cow a ticking off for flying off the handle in the first place, by implying that she was showing her knickers deliberately.

Of course this type of situation does offer plenty of other possibilities. Supposing that the chap had really been eyeing her up, the episode with the knickers would give him a perfect reason for trying his luck with her. Then of course he'd have to answer her tirade with something ingratiating like:

'Look, I'm terribly sorry. I know this must look like the most awful pick-up, but I couldn't help noticing you standing by the chocolate machine and I'm afraid I couldn't help seeing that you were having some trouble with your underwear. Please excuse my apparent rudeness, but I was only trying to save your embarrassment. Could I apologize properly over a cup of coffee/a drink/ dinner sometime/ in Marks while you're buying another pair?'

Apart from his cowering subservience and his subtly boyish

manner the man who can produce a reply like this also has the presence of mind to swap 'knickers' for the more decorous 'underwear' – which shows that he's got breeding. Even if his amorous intentions prove fruitless, he's certainly far less likely to be slapped across the face for his pains.

Anyhow, that's quite enough about knickers. The point is that delicate conversations can occur any time and anywhere. They creep up on us unexpectedly and trip us up if we're not careful. Even if we can't prevent ourselves from falling, we can at least take care that we fall properly and do ourselves the minimum of damage.

So for the sake of simplicity, I have divided the various types of delicate conversations into three broad areas – affairs of the heart, criticism, and awkward and embarrassing situations.

Here goes.

Affairs of the Heart

Without doubt the most important of these is falling in love.

People have been falling in love ever since Adam and Eve, but the formulae of how it happens are as complicated and varied as those that they print on the side of bottles of mineral water. But falling in love is one thing. The real problem is getting the message across, and this is where conversation comes in.

I have always believed that true love is founded on understanding. That may sound like a platitude, probably because it is, but if you get completely the wrong idea of what the other person feels about you right from the start, then things can become horribly confused later on.

If you gaze into a pair of limpid eyes on the Central Line at 5.35 every week-day evening, your tactics clearly must be very different from those of the country swain who has been courting for two years and eventually plucks up courage to pop the question having found out that he won't stand a cat in hell's chance of getting an estate cottage unless he's married.

Making an advance to an absolute stranger is by far the most difficult; about the only advantage it has in fact is the element of surprise. I knew a bloke who had once been asked by a gorgeous cinema usherette, 'Can I show you to your seat, sir?' to which he replied, with great presence of mind, 'Thanks, but I'd far rather be shown to yours.' And he was!

In spite of the inroads of the women's lib brigade, it's still mainly men who have to take it upon themselves to utter the magic words. That's fine if you come from south of Brussels, but for the rest of us it's not that easy. Though speaking of magic words, don't let yourself get off on the wrong foot by an approach like the one overheard to a pretty waitress in a tea-shop:

'Would you like me to whisper to you the three words every girl longs to hear?'

'Yes'.

'Here's your tip.'

Likewise the tired old phrases like, 'Has anyone told you that you're beautiful?', or, 'You must get used to being told that you're an amazingly attractive girl', are only useful opening gambits if they share some connection with reality. If they don't they come out as rather unimaginative flattery. Of course they also leave themselves open to the simple rebuff, 'yes'.

Love strikes us at the most inopportune moment. A colleague of mine was pierced by Cupid's arrow just as a district nurse was dressing his backside following an operation he'd had for a colourful complaint called 'Jeep seat'. There's not a lot you can do to help your cause when you're flat on your face with a pretty girl pouring TCP and baby powder over your bum. He had the idea of asking her out for dinner, but somehow that didn't seem very suitable under the circumstances. So he decided to ask her swimming because that would be good physiotherapy, but in the middle of February that suggestion didn't work out as well as he hoped.

There must be something about women in uniforms that turns on some men. Nurses I can understand, ministering angels and all that, but policewomen, that does take some understanding. But one man's poison is another man's meat, so to speak, though in one instance that springs to mind the two were combined.

I still maintain, mind you, that the driver threw caution to the winds, for he had two endorsements already, but it still took some courage to pick up the officer who was booking him. He was just cruising gently through a 30 mph limit minding his own business at about 45 (well, we all do, don't we?) when a girl popped out from behind a wooden fence and waved him to the side of the road. For one ghastly minute he thought that he'd run over someone and not stopped, and the look on his face must have given him away immediately. But the girl seemed a bit unsure of herself too.

'Excuse me, sir,' she said through the window which was firmly closed. 'Excuse me, sir. Would you mind opening your window and turning off your radio.'

Which the driver duly did.

'I have to inform you that anything you may say – no, sorry, that comes later. I have to inform you that you were picked up on the radar travelling at 46 miles-per-hour in a 30 mile-an-hour limit. I have to warn you that anything you say may be taken down and may be used in evidence against you. Do you have anything to say?'

Quite sensibly the driver said that he had not and the policewoman then asked to see his driving licence and copied down the number of the car. She wrote something down on a piece of paper, tore it up and tried to write it down again. At the third attempt she started to blush and the façade cracked. She started to giggle.

After warning him that he would be receiving a summons in due course she told him that he could drive on and he was just about to pull away when she dashed out from the pavement again saying:

'Oh, wait a minute. I didn't write down your address.'

'I didn't write down yours,' said the driver, 'but I got your number. How about letting me book you one evening?' And the jammy devil did. Mind you his summons came through the post just the same, and he lost his licence.

Then there are those circumstances which are almost too opportune, like finding yourself standing next to the ideal stranger while you're peering into the window of a sex-shop. There's no point in trying to disguise what you're up to. That runs the terrible risk of giving the idea that you're less than normal. All you can do is to brazen it out, bearing in mind that whoever you're interested in is looking at the same window.

'Excuse me. I'm intrigued by that thing there (pointing at some weird appliance fitted with wires and straps), do you have any idea what it's for?', is probably as good a way of getting off the ground as any other. And if you strike lucky and she does know what it's for then you'll probably get on like a house on fire.

There are times of course when the interest can be mutual. I remember a friend of mine pulling into a petrol station to buy some fuel in the days before self-service pumps. It was during a heat-wave and the staff at the garage were wearing bathing costumes and very little else. He's a pretty average sort of a bloke, but almost every woman I speak to talks about his 'smouldering looks' or his 'burning eyes', or something like that. Anyway, whatever he had did something to the girl filling his tank, and when he went up to the counter to pay she leaned across at him threateningly and said, 'How would you like to fill my tank – tiger.' If he hadn't already been late for a vital golf-match, I dread to think what might have happened. Which simply proves my point that love, infatuation, call it what you will, can creep up on us all at the least expected opportunity.

Sensing the emotion is one thing of course. Actually making the right words come out of your mouth is quite another matter, as all of us who have stammered our way through interminable adolescent formulae know to our cost.

The real point about saying 'I love you' to a total stranger is its suddenness. Play on this for all its worth. Although most people haven't any time for love at first sight, there's always the exception that proves the rule, and that exception is usually the chap who can do the whole thing convincingly and with sufficient romantic flair so that he just succeeds in sounding sincere instead of sounding like a waiter on the Costa del Sol.

Fictional characters always have it so easy, which probably explains why actors have become pastmasters at the art, after rubbing shoulders, so to speak, with all the great lovers of litera-ture.

Lovers in plays and books start off with two big advantages over we lesser mortals. Their conversation is always pre-planned and it always comes from better-than-average brains. How many of us could cross our hearts and honestly admit that we could go up to a girl in a disco, always assuming that we could make ourselves heard, and say:

> If I profane with my unworthiest hand
> This holy shrine, the gentle sin is this.
> My lips two blushing pilgrims stand
> To smooth the rough touch with a loving kiss.

Mind you, how many girls could come up with an answer like:

> Good pilgrim, you do wrong your hand too much,
> Which mannerly devotion shows in this.
> For saints have hands that pilgrims' hands do touch
> And palm to palm is holy palmers' kiss.

Having said this, though, it's only fair to point out that I am an incurable optimist when it comes to affairs of the heart. I honestly believe that if we accept our limitations, which isn't always easy or palatable, there is no reason why we shouldn't display the same reverence as Romeo, or the same encouragement as Juliet. If you try to say 'I love you' to a total stranger you're always going to run the risk of sounding corny whatever you say. But if you can say it with enough conviction and let the force of your feelings shine through the words, then anyone remotely interested will see that you are sincere and will overlook the clichés that might accidentally slip in in the heat of the moment.

The trouble is that so few of us willingly admit to having any limitations when it comes to our prowess as Don Juans. Even if we make some faltering attempts at self-analysis, we usually get it hopelessly wrong.

I've seen middle-aged, balding accountants holding hands with their secretaries in dimly-lit, grossly-overpriced restaurants whispering things like: 'I never realized I could be so happy. I know you won't believe me when I tell you this, but the moment I saw you walk into the office I felt myself slipping, and now there's no stopping me. I'm terribly afraid that I've fallen head over heels in love with you.'

That sort of stuff brings a blush to my cheeks and quite puts me off my sweetbreads, never mind what it does to the sweet young thing who is only on the look-out for a sugar-daddy. The poor old chap, who's probably been rehearsing those lines for a week on the 8.15 from Dorking, would have been far better off offering her an allowance of £3,000 a year and a discreet flat for two in Maida Vale. But then he probably couldn't have afforded it. Love and romance are full of pitfalls for the unwary.

When I was learning the rudiments of courting, the 'angry young man' approach was going down very well. There seemed to be brooding Jimmy Porters hovering in every bar, in old jackets, with pale, but interesting, boyish features, a perpetual scowl, a copy of the *New Statesman* jutting out of a side-pocket, and a pint of Guinness and a packet of ten of the cheapest cigarettes on the table.

The lines would go something like this:

'I don't care what you think. You'll probably laugh in my face, I would if anyone said this to me. I don't expect you to feel the same about me. I don't expect you to be aware of me at all in fact, why should you? I hate the word love. That's why I never use it. But there's something about you which disturbs me so much that I won't get any peace unless we do something about it. Do you want another half . . .?'

This may be a far cry from the elegant quatrains of Shakespeare's star-struck lovers, but then John Travolta and William Kemp don't share a lot in common as actors, but they seemed to do quite well in their respective ages.

Of course if you really are sincere in your feelings, and your intentions are therefore entirely honourable, it's disastrous to blurt out anything like: 'You're the first girl I've ever really loved – so please go to bed with me.'

That's probably a perfectly accurate statement of the way you feel, but take my word for it, approaches like that simply fall between two stools. In the first place, if what you say is intended solely as an expression of a genuine, burning affection, why complicate things by introducing what is after all a natural follow-on, always assuming that your beloved shares your feelings and you have just enough patience to let the thing decently mature?

On the other hand if, as is far more likely, your intentions are anything but honourable, then your approach needs to set off on very different tack. There's no point in beating about the bush. Once you've made up your mind, get on with it, otherwise the anxiety will kill you both.

It seems to me that you'll almost inevitably be rebuffed, it's all part of the game, but apart from being prepared for that, there's precious little that you can do about it. There are only really two strategies that have ever worked with this type of approach, the cunningly suggestive, or the brazenly down-to-earth. Take a deep breath and start talking, making whatever you say short and to the point.

Mind you, I never had the courage or the imagination to put this sort of thing into practice myself, but I suppose I've always had a secret yearning to have a go at it. But a page from my note-book gives a few of the lines which I've either overheard, or had suggested to me by semi-paralytic advisers, who've probably got even less nerve than me.

Here they are, for someone's future reference, even if they've outlived their usefulness for me:

'The same God that put these feelings inside me isn't going to turn round and tell me they're wrong, just because we're not married.'

(Following some gentle physical contact): 'These are only whispers, but wait till I shout at you.'

'I feel so frustrated. I think there must be something wrong with me. Will you help me get over it?'

'I'm frightened that I'm gay. Help me prove to myself that I'm not.'

'I've never done it before either, so we can experience something new together.'

'Don't worry. Of course I'll still respect you in the morning.'

'It doesn't make sense for me to go now, since it's already three-thirty and we're going for a walk at eight.'

'I've known you long enough. So if you don't say 'yes' tonight, you can just forget about it.'

'I don't want to get anything out of you. I just want you to enjoy it too.'

'If you really love me then prove it.'

Once you're over the first hurdle everything is plain sailing

69

until the affair turns sour and one of you has to bail out – and this is where conversations can be really delicate!

In my more cynical moments I've often pondered the reason for marriage. It occurs to me during these dark nights of the soul that one of the principal reasons for people staying married is the fact that they can't bear the emotional turmoil of going through the bust-up. Still, the alarming divorce statistics today show that many people do eventually decide that enough is enough – and say so.

But, as with everything else to do with conversation, there are ways of saying what you mean, and ways *not* to say what you mean. I know of a chap who calmly told his wife one Friday morning at breakfast that he was leaving her for another woman after twelve years of relatively stable married life. She hadn't even had an inkling of what was coming. But what made the situation even more unfeeling was that he seemed genuinely put out when she dissolved into tears instead of cooking his breakfast.

Though quite what you do say once you've successfully passed the seven-year-itch and then decide you've made a mistake, I haven't the faintest idea.

Telling someone that you don't love them after all is the hardest form of truth, particularly if you like them. If you don't give a damn then it's really quite easy, you can just be insulting and leave it at that.

One celebrated old roué from my youth used to play deliberately on his reputation whenever he wanted to disentangle himself from one doting female and get involved with another. He used to take them to the same restaurant night after night, sit them at the same table and order the same dishes every time. Why he did not arrange for the same music to be played I don't know, but perhaps he might have felt that that was going too far. After hinting darkly during the meal that something was on his mind he used to wait for the coffee before spilling the beans.

'You know how much you mean to me,' he would begin, with just a hint of regret in his voice. 'You know how much we have enjoyed being together for [and it could vary from six hours to six months]. But now we have reached a crossroads. Selfishly I wanted you to turn and come with me. But seeing you here, I realize that I have no right to ask you to sacrifice yourself to a man with a reputation such as mine. I cannot drag you down with me, my dear. I cannot ask you to waste yourself. Our love has been a beautiful thing, I cannot allow myself to taint it. We must part. You will love other men, I can tell. I will be seen with other women, I know. But they will only be substitutes for what you have meant to me.'

Then he would quickly get up and leave, overcome by emotion, before his beloved had a chance willingly to offer herself to redeem him. Towards the end of his career he even arranged to have a taxi waiting outside to take him off to his next conquest waiting in another restaurant, out of harm's way.

Just for the record, I once had a lady friend who was just as effective in getting rid of her suitors without even having to raise the unpleasant subject of their parting. Her policy revolved around dinner, too, though this one she prepared herself. She used to serve the same meal, cream of mushroom soup, dover sole, chicken supreme and any soufflé, as long as it was white. She took care to dress entirely in white as well, and to finish the ensemble the meal was served on a plain linen table cloth, laid with plain white plates and ivory-handled cutlery. This has absolutely nothing to do with conversation of course, but the effect of all this virginal white was more than enough to quench even the most obstinate admirer's ardour.

Times have changed and sensibilities have changed with them to such an extent that most of this beating about the bush can be done away with – which is probably no bad thing, except when it comes to tackling prospective in-laws. I know of several happy marriages which almost failed to get off the ground after some unguarded remark to a future parent-in-law.

One chap in particular was getting along terribly well with his girlfriend's mother, which came as a surprise to them both considering that she was strictly teetotal and he was the complete opposite. It's only fair to mention that the good lady's offspring were partial to a drop or two, in fact that was how the happy couple met in the first place. But during the course of their chat my chum had downed more than was prudent under the circumstances, and when he noticed that his hostess was refusing wine and only drinking mineral water he asked why this was:

'Well, I never drink alcohol,' she told him demurely.

'What,' he said without thinking. 'You bring up a family of alcoholics and don't touch a drop yourself . . .', only to be silenced with a withering glance. If he hadn't already popped the question and been accepted, that could have ended the affair there and then.

Others have gone to opposite extreme, which can damage their chances almost as much. The daughter of a well-known university professor took her intended home one weekend to stay at the family's country home. The poor boyfriend knew of her parents by reputation and was terrified of putting his foot in it. So he spent the whole week-end calling her old man 'Sir' and opening doors for her mother, which ironically cut right across the parents' attempts at being carefree and Bohemian. By the time Sunday tea came round everyone was on edge, especially the boyfriend who realized that he was in the wrong, but in his panic could not see why.

'Do you want milk and sugar, Roger,' the lady of the house asked him.

'Two lumps of sugar, please, your ladyship, but no milk – if it's no bother.'

'It's no trouble to me,' she told him wearily,' I just don't put the milk in.'

And as if that wasn't bad enough he compounded his embarrassment by trying to perch a buttered scone on the rim of his cup while he reached for the raspberry jam, and only succeeded in nudging the scone into the Earl Grey and slopping it all over the elegant, raw-silk upholstery. He was never invited again.

There's a character in Christopher Hampton's play, *The Philanthropist*, called Liz, who appears in the dinner-party scene and

doesn't say a word. In the meantime everyone else is desperately trying to score emotional points and get themselves fixed up for the evening, in some cases, and for longer in others. But as it turns out Liz gets her man, and is the only one who's successful.

If it's true that the course of true love never does run smooth, perhaps the best policy with affairs of the heart is to stay quiet and sit tight when all about you are losing theirs.

Criticism

Critics are to actors what the last remaining tufts of hair are to a bald man. They point up our inadequacies and shortcomings on a superficial level, mocking us in the eyes of the world at large, without offering any constructive help for improving things. But once they lose interest in us and disappear, our fortunes wane and we look even less appealing to the general public.

Critics have to be suffered and endured, like journalists and reporters. But I find it's best to be philosophical about what they have to say. If you get a notice that you think is unjustified, always try and forget it. After all nothing is deader than yesterday's news and many critics criticize not the play as it is presented, but the play as they would like to present it themselves.

This is a terrible annoyance of course, though, even so, we've usually been able to pinch a few quotes from them in the past which look good outside the theatre. And that's often the only way that actors can get their own back, by quoting the critics out of context. It's really quite immoral, but all's fair in love and war – mostly war – I suppose.

The trouble with criticism in show business is that it usually appears in print. Actors seldom get a chance to have a go at the critics in the flesh. This has its compensations, though, because the things one would like to say sometimes wouldn't do one any good in the popularity stakes by the time the paper comes out.

For this reason there is really no way of going one up on a reporter. You really have to go one down to go one up, as Stephen Potter so rightly said. If you meet a reporter, and some of them are pretty disastrous personalities by the nature of their extraordinary work, you can't remonstrate or be too arrogant with them, for the simple reason that they can always get back at you in print, especially if they work for a popular paper with a very large audience which likes nothing better than to see you put down.

So my policy is always to try to be nice to them and to try not to hang about with them for too long either. The only tiresome thing which I find with some reporters is that at the end of a rather long interview they reach for their battered briefcases and bring out scripts for pilot comedy series, which they hope I'm going to star in. Most of them, bless their hearts, seem to be playwrights *manqués*, searching for a producer.

Criticism from other quarters can be dealt with more positively, though this isn't always the case, especially when it comes from fans. I remember being in *The Wild Duck* at the Lyric, Hammersmith in which I was called upon to knock myself out in five exhausting acts. One night after the play I arrived in the bar, still panting and sweating from my efforts, merely to be told by one of the three or four faithful fans who get to know one rather too well, 'that was very nice'. I had another drink and remembered *Whose Life Is It Anyway?* Just then I thought I wouldn't mind spending the whole of *The Wild Duck* sitting propped up in bed. With fans like that, who needs enemies?

What can be even more galling is the criticism from directors or fellow-actors which you know is wrong, or quite irrelevant. I love the story of the wonderful old ham cast in a rep production of *Macbeth*. The director had seen Macbeth as a man suffering an inferiority complex and had blocked out his movements as those of a nervous, frightened maniac – a sort of cross between Mole in *The Wind in the Willows* and Adolf Hitler. However, the lead had very different ideas and throughout rehearsals he and the director were constantly contradicting each other about the interpretation of the part. When the first night came they had established a sort of uneasy truce. But the sight of a full house sent the blood to the old boy's head and when it came to 'Is this a dagger etc.' the blocking went to pieces along with the cowering nervousness of the first act. He started to charge about the stage, declaiming like one of the three weird sisters, and finally backed off-stage through the castle gate through which Macduff was about to enter, leaving himself on the wrong side for his next entry.

The director had been watching from the wings and was apoplectic with rage. He tore into Macbeth in scarcely muffled curses and abuse, but the only response he got was a stentorian reply, which rang around the house and silenced Lady Macbeth, who had just got to the bit about drugging the groom's possets:

'If it was good enough for Wolfit, young man, it's certainly good enough for you.'

Oh to have that confidence and that command!

One of the problems with playing the sort of characters I portray is that everyone expects me to behave like that in real life. In some ways it's quite helpful as I get into trouble by nature and the people in Marks & Sparks think it's hilarious if I get anything wrong or forget my money, so I'm usually spared any criticism, if not embarrassment.

But there are times when being Tom Good to most people backfires. I remember an incident with a taxi driver only too vividly which brought this point home to me. I was in a desperate hurry to get to my destination and like a fool I'd decided to go by car because I thought it would save time. There was something on, the Cup Final maybe, because the roads were thick with traffic. After waiting to pull into the endless stream of cars I eventually saw a taxi slowing down, to let me out, as I thought. So I pulled out smartly, just in front of him as it turned out, and gave him a cheery wave of thanks as I drove past.

But the taxi-driver had slammed on his brakes and the passenger, for whom he was stopping, had been pitched onto the floor of the cab and was kneeling on the floor looking daggers at me out of the window:

'Why don't you stick to your f***ing tractor,' the driver yelled out, 'or the goat.'

I drove on, blushing to my socks, and, watching the road intently thereafter, nearly knocked a nun off a zebra-crossing.

If I can give myself a pat on the back for anything, it's probably for being fairly punctual, so I don't often get ticked off for being late. But I know lots of people who make a habit of being late just to exercise their skill in getting out of it.

There was a chap working in a studio with me who always seemed to disappear for a couple of hours for his lunch break. At first people didn't mind too much, but when this became a regular habit, he was taken aside and told to buck up his ideas:

'Why should you take twice as long over lunch as anyone else?' he was asked.

'Probably because I eat twice as much,' he answered and

swanned off. He didn't stay to enjoy many more canteen lunches, though.

Knowing how to give criticism, however, is just as much of an art as being able to take it. There are some types of criticism which border on the insult. I've overheard some pretty choice remarks addressed to barbers while I've been waiting round the partition reading last month's *Mayfair*.

'I wanted a trim, not a nibble,' said one irate retired military man, after a pimply assistant had tried to improve upon what was already a very severe short back and sides. While at the other extreme came the anguished cry of, 'Do I get a refund if you take off all the hair,' which emanated from one shaggy youth whose father had brought him in for a hair cut before going back to school.

I've always fought shy of antagonizing barbers, though. Memories of Sweeney Todd and half-remembered ideas that barbers might once have been surgeons have usually stifled my annoyance, at least until I have been standing upright once again and able to fend for myself.

Besides I take exception to those people who imagine that because they are customers they have carte blanche to abuse the staff. 'Speak as you would be spoken to' has always seemed a perfectly reasonable maxim, that like all perfectly reasonable maxims is easy to say and jolly hard to stick to.

Criticism when it is directed at one's peers or one's family is quite a different matter and here I can be as trenchant as the next man. The mother of a friend of mine had a wonderful way of registering approval or disapproval of her daughter's friends when they telephoned. If she liked them she would come and say, 'So-and-so is on the phone for you, dear.' If she didn't like them the message would come out as either, 'Your friend, so-and-so, is on the phone', or 'That so-and-so is on the phone.' Anyone branded as, 'your friend, that Richard' was way beyond the pale in that house at least.

Criticism to an actor of course means something very different to criticism addressed, say, to a private in the army. A Sergeant-Major's criticism is seldom constructive, at least in the short term, whereas all actors cherish the secret hope that critics might even help them to improve, or might even praise their work.

I remember falling into this trap with Noel Coward – the trap about praise that is. Coward had been to see me in *Present Laughter* and he told me afterwards: 'You know, you really are one of our best farcers', and then he paused. I was waiting for the great accolade to tell my children, the praise which Noel Coward had given to my wonderful work and my remarkable talent, and he then continued, 'You never ever hang about.'

Well, it could have been a great deal worse, even if it was a bit of a let down at the time, but as Somerset Maugham wrote in *Of Human Bondage*: 'People ask you for criticism, but they only want praise.'

Awkward or Embarrassing Situations

I never believe those people who maintain that they never find themselves in awkward or embarrassing situations. Either they're lying or they're not human, or in some circumstances both.

I think there are two distinct types of awkward or embarrassing situations. You may feel just as terrible in both of them, but in one case the embarrassment is usually your own, while in the other you feel embarrassed for the other person, if you follow my meaning. The first type arises from trying to get someone else to do something for you. The second comes from trying to do something for someone else.

Bank managers seem to be prime culprits in the first case. I've come to the conclusion that all the terrible traumas that we go through in visiting the inner sanctum to look blankly at our balance sheets and have a lecture on living within our means are quite unnecessary. The simple truth is that there's really nothing to talk about. If we're in trouble the bank manager can't help us anyway, and if we've got money in the bank all he can do is bow and scrape. So going to see him is really a waste of time, especially in our present economic climate. But this does not prevent us from dutifully trudging along to ask if we can borrow enough to buy a new mowing machine, or pay the garage to change the oil in the car.

Some people, however, seem to have got it down to a fine art, like the ones who spend half their lives filling in Social Security forms and living like lords on the proceeds. They and the bank manager share a *lingua franca* which the rest of us catch snippets of from the business pages of the daily paper and *The Financial World Tonight* on the radio.

They breeze into the manager's office with an air of calm authority, sit down before being invited to and then launch into a five-minute synopsis of what they want and why they want it, sprinkling their monologue with phrases like 'critical path analysis', 'double taxation relief', and 'watered stock'.

I don't have a clue what half of it means, and I'm pretty sure that the common or garden bank manager doesn't know either. But where it doesn't matter if I show my ignorance, the manager stands to lose face if he appears anything but totally au fait with what is being said.

So after the tirade is finished, there is a respectable pause, designed to show that some deliberation is taking place, and the bank manager then mutters something like:

'Well, you must appreciate that under the present circumstances we have to be rather careful of how we dispose of our assets. But in view of what you've told me, I don't see that there should be any reason to prevent us agreeing to what you have asked for. Shall we say fifty thousand now and fifty thousand in six months? This will involve an adjustment to the rates of course. Well I think that covers everything – Do come and see me at any time.'

FRED JONES
1879-1948
AND HIS WIFE
ENID
1880-1949
STILL NOT
TALKING TO
EACH OTHER
UP
ABOVE

They shake hands, agree to have a round of golf soon and the manager goes back to doing his crossword while the client goes off to settle the hire purchase on his Rolls.

Doctors have a similar aura surrounding them. There's a line in *Hamlet* which says, 'There's such divinity doth hedge a king' which I've always thought could be applied to doctors, if you swapped 'obscurity' for 'divinity' and 'doctor' for 'king'.

Doctors can be embarrassing either because they chat airily about parts of our anatomy using menacing words which we have never heard before, or because they chat about our bodies in ways that are all too easy to understand:

'You say you want me to give you a life insurance report? I say you'd be better off paying into a funeral fund. You smoke forty a day, you drink an average of eight pints a night, you're five stone overweight and you insist on jogging every morning.'

Going to the doctor can be a wretched business, too, even if you're just going for simple treatment, and doctors aren't always the most sympathetic when it comes to helping their patients out of some dilemmas.

'Which would you prefer me to get, a tin-opener or a hacksaw,' one harrassed casualty doctor asked a man who had somehow got his thumb stuck in a six-foot length of copper piping and was sitting in the casualty department, surrounded by the Saturday night drunks and the last of the rugger injuries, with his appendage sticking up in the air like a radio mast.

'Don't worry Doc, just plug the other end into the mains, that should get me out,' said the patient with a cheerful grin, putting the doctor well and truly in his place.

People in shops can be awkward sometimes as well, though as I mentioned earlier I have a built-in excuse for making an ass of myself. I reserve the greatest sympathy for all those unfortunates who want to try to change unwanted Christmas presents, just as the shops are in the teeth of the January sales.

The classic case of this of course is Bob Newhart's episode with an unwanted toupée. Fortunately I've never been given an unwanted hat, never mind a hair-piece, but there have been times when I have had to dispose of unwanted presents, and trying to take them back to the shops has to be the final resort.

What do you do with a full-length body stocking sent by a well-meaning viewer of *The Good Life*, 'to keep out the chill when you're working in that muddy garden in the winter'? The label showed where it had come from, which was one consolation. If it had been one of the mail-order firms, taking it back to the shops would have been a non-starter. It was also clear from the colour and size of the gift that it would have been better suited for Mrs Good than for me.

The shop seemed to be full of women fitting themselves out for trips to the Antarctic. There were socks of every length and design, strange body garments with bits hanging down at the back and boasting phrases like 'double-thickness', 'hygienic and comfortable' and 'as worn on Everest', and my pale-green creation displayed in all its glory on a ridiculously slim dummy in the window.

'I wonder if I could exchange this?' I asked, in the hope that no one would overhear.

'I think we might be able to arrange it,' whispered the middle-aged assistant, giving me a coy wink.

'I can see why you wouldn't want to be seen in this,' she continued, opening out the entire garment across the counter in full view of the whole shop, 'They'd have to call it the *Ghoul Life!*' Helpless giggling broke out from all parts of the shop floor.

After that experience I have taken to disposing of my unwanted presents in a less conspicuous way. What I usually do at Christmas is to rewrap them very quickly, put them in a cupboard and then give them to people I don't like very much the following Christmas. This has always worked well and has never caused any problems, except for one notable exception when I inadvertently gave a present back to the person who had given it to me the year before, still in the same paper.

What really makes perfectly natural situations embarrassing is the way that other people seem to take exception to what we say.

Asking people to stop doing something which is clearly unnecessary or in some cases not allowed always seems to put their backs up, no matter how tactful you try to be.

I've asked people before now not to smoke in No Smoking areas, and received some very colourful replies. Yet there are others who can make their point far more effectively and with the minimum of embarrassment to themselves. I have always admired the sangfroid of a lady passenger I read of who was travelling in a No Smoking car of *The Flying Scotsman* when she was joined by a bluff Glaswegian who sat down opposite her, took out a revolting, old pipe and started to light it up as he asked,

'Yu dunna mind ef I smook?'

'Not in the slightest,' the good lady replied,' as long as you don't mind me being sick.'

Another perfectly reasonable complaint which seems to be more in evidence than ever is the short measure controversy. The snag I find, however, is that the barman who pulls you three-quarters of a pint and 'a good head', also happens to look like an ex-Royal Marine commando. Pleasant approaches like, 'Now then, mine host, I'll have the weights and measures chappies on to you,' or 'Sorry to be a nuisance, but I think the barrels still a bit lively,' don't get you anywhere. The barman either turns nasty and asks you to leave, or else he asks if you want to make an issue of it, and what was intended as a quiet drink after a tiring day turns into a defence of your virility.

The sort of comment which shows that you're capable of giving as good as you get is the one which catches the barman off his guard:

'Excuse me, can you put a whisky in this?'

'Certainly sir.'

'Well, in that case would you mind filling up with beer.'

And then there is the one which I have always longed to have the nerve to use.

'How's business these days?'

'Not so good, you know. People are coming in less than they

used to, especially during the week. Well there isn't the money around, what with Christmas, and the recession and everything.'

'You'd like it then if you could sell a bit more beer.'

'Too right I would.'

'Well, why not try selling less froth then.'

Experience has taught me that you've got to have very small barmen attending to you before you try anything like that.

I've given up drinking expensive wine in restaurants for similar reasons, and now we always drink the house wine. You need about £16 to get a decent bottle of wine in a restaurant these days and when you can buy it round the corner at your local liquormarket for half the price it really isn't worth spending the money in a restaurant. This is especially true if you actually notice what you're being served.

I've seen people getting into the most awful rows with waiters when they've tried to send back wine which they thought was the wrong temperature, or in one case the wrong bottle. But you've got to be jolly sure of what you're doing if you do decide to take on the headwaiter of any restaurant with pretentions to haute cuisine.

I was sitting alongside a chap who was having a blazing row with the wine waiter over a bottle of fairly costly claret which he had ordered. This chap had evidently been told that the wine should have been served at room temperature, and as far as he was concerned it wasn't. The conversation was gradually dying throughout the rest of the restaurant, as it always does when this sort of thing starts up. The head-waiter hurried over to see what all the fuss was about and when he got the wine-waiter's version he gave the customer a look of complete and utter disdain and imperiously said:

'You must excuse the misunderstanding, sir. But in view of the fact that you ordered this with the truite meunière, it was rather confusing as to which temperature you wished the wine to be served at.'

If the customer had not made himself so objectionable in the first place, the waiter might have been kinder, he might even have

been embarrassed for the poor man, who had made a perfectly reasonable choice, even if it did flout the best gourmet conventions.

Feeling bad on other people's account can be just as wretched as being acutely embarrassed yourself. An actor friend of mine went along to a barber to get a Roman haircut after he had been cast in a production of *Julius Caesar*. The style interested the young man cutting his hair and they got talking about it.

'I'm an actor you see,' explained my friend, 'and the next play I'm in is set in ancient Rome so I've got to look like a Roman, you know, short at the front. At least you're using scissors. I read somewhere that originally they had their hair singed.'

'What play's that then,' the barber asked him.

'*Julius Caesar*.'

'Who wrote that then?'

'Well, Shakespeare actually,' my friend told him after a slight pause.

'Oh God . . . of course,' said the barber, crestfallen.

My chum felt so awkward he ended up giving him his two complimentary tickets.

Twice I've tried to help out people I've seen walking towards me with their flies wide open, merely because of the profound debt of gratitude I owe to a huge, black guard on the underground who saw me in this state once and yelled out with a beaming smile: 'Oh dear, man, de flies is all undone!'

Here again, though, my approach was essentially far too timid and as it turned out far too misleading. I tried to attract the first man's attention silently as he was walking towards me by making furtive movements towards my crutch. But he didn't catch on straightaway and as we drew nearer I started to feel very self-conscious. In the end I broke my silence and whispered to him as he passed me:

'Did you know your flies are undone?'

'Yes,' he said, 'But what am I supposed to do about it when the zip's bust?'

The second time was really even more alarming as the unfortunate man in question was foreign and his command of English did not extend to trouser fittings.

'Your flies are undone,' I told him, giving up mime for a bad job.

'No. I come by ship to Duver,' he told me confidently.

'No. Your zipper is undone,' I persisted.

'Yes, shipper,' he said slightly bemused.

Eventually restored to making rapid up-and-down movements with my hands indicating what he should do. His trousers were fitted with buttons and I don't think he really understood what I had been telling him because he was still muttering, 'Very good shippers' as he did himself up and walked off in the opposite direction.

Come to think of it, his might have been the best policy after all.

He didn't seem the least bit put out by being told that he was about to expose himself, and I certainly finished by far the most embarrassed of the two. After all, if the good Samaritan had found that the man lying by the road worked for the *Candid Camera* team, he, too, would have felt a right Charlie.

Maybe the best way to deal with awkward or embarrassing situations is just to ignore them. Certainly from my own experience the more you try to settle them by conversation the worse they become. On the other hand a more charitable approach might be to know how to kill them before they get too horribly out of control.

5

Halt!

conversation stoppers

I think somebody once said that the only good conversation was a dead one, and even if they didn't say it, they probably should have done. This may strike you as being pessimistic, but believe me there have been times in my life, as there are in most people's lives, when I would quite happily have disappeared in a cloud of smoke had the magic lamp been at hand. As it was, I had to resort to killing the conversation before it got too appallingly out of hand.

Conversations tend to get out of our control for one perfectly simple reason, namely that more than one person takes part in them. Monologues are really far safer ground in this respect.

Provided you can martial your thoughts into some semblance of order before you get going, there's no reason why you shouldn't natter away for minutes on end without the slightest risk of anything going wrong. The trouble starts when other people try to butt in. They call it 'contributing', but don't be misled. It's a takeover bid.

Let someone else join in and you immediately lose the controlling share in the conversation. Allow more than one other to start speaking and your stake drops to that of a minority shareholder. All you then need is for some twit to take exception to what you're saying and the whole fabric of your beautifully structured dialogue begins to crumble.

Worse still is what happens when you've had a few. I used to find that I was always at my most eloquent, and talkative, when the demon vino had got to work. But the same devil also made me highly indignant when I was confronted in full flight. I never got to the point of exchanging blows with anyone, but I said some pretty heated things until I learned how to win a conversation by simply cutting it off in mid-stream.

There are times, too, when you have to deliver the coup de grâce to your own best bon mot, or raciest anecdote, after realizing that you're on the verge of putting your foot well and truly in it.

It comes as little comfort to learn that experts in conversation can be just as artless at times. During the Lancaster House conference on Rhodesian independence there was a potentially very awkward moment when one junior foreign office official, in his cups, commented to a black reporter that he and his kind really

CONVERSATION STOPPER (No!)

were Ian Smith's *bêtes noirs*. He was of course referring to the press and that loose federation dubbed the media. At least his black chum had the wit to reply that tactless oafs like he and his kind were the white man's burden, otherwise the course of history might have taken a very different turn.

Still that's what diplomacy is all about – telling people to get knotted elegantly, eloquently and with the minimum of fuss. And a person who can genuinely call himself a diplomat is one who, in Caskie Stinett's well-turned phrase from *Out of the Red*, 'can tell you to go to hell in such a way that you actually look forward to the trip'.

Conversations occasionally come to a halt by themselves and moments like these should be cherished if you happen to be speaking at the time, because as every politician, and Mrs Thatcher's speech-writer, have come to realize, pauses lend weight to what is being said.

I've found myself listening in awe to someone rambling on about a subject about which I know next to nothing, only to be riveted by some astonishing remark which leaves everyone gasping with amazement. That's the best kind of conversation stopper, the one I always strive for, the one that brings respect and reputation as a raconteur and sage.

As luck, or fate, would have it, however, I have been cast in a different role, with which only time and painful experience have helped me come to terms. My only consolation is that almost everyone I know plays the same part, and those few who assume the air of calm authority are too unmentionably priggish even to get into conversation with. I am of course referring to the time-honoured habit of Briers and mankind to go charging through life's conversations with the same carefree abandon of a 'chinaman in a bullshop', as one of my dearest friends and fellow sufferers puts it.

The results of this sort of activity are always amusing in retrospect, which, if it's any consolation, make them good anecdote material, but at the time they are dreadfully humiliating for all concerned.

I remember chatting to an actress friend of mine some time ago about her actor husband who was, to say the least, far less successful than his wife. She told me that he had moved to St George's and I jumped in, rather patronizingly, to say, 'Well, I think that's marvellous. I think he's so wise to get out of the business and do something really worthwhile, working in hospital as an orderly.'

'Not the hospital, Richard,' she told me tartly, 'St George's Theatre.'

If predicaments like that seem bad enough there is one category even further down the road to social ruin, when words themselves cease to be of any use and we have to rely on imagination for our salvation.

I've known grown men invent the most complicated ruses for escaping from conversations that have landed them in hot water and I've known others who have thrown up their hands in despair and fallen in a dead faint instead. These are the physical conversation stoppers, the ones which we have to keep tucked out of sight, like the cyanide pill, to be used when all else fails.

That may sound a little dramatic, but it's worth bearing in mind that these sort of things can't be used more than once, if you have any designs on staying part of the human race, that is. After all, who want's to get a reputation for collapsing with a suspected coronary every time he compliments a woman on her fine grandson only to be told that she's the child's mother?

Well, that's the scenario. Conversation stoppers are like a car's brakes, they keep us on a safe course if we're careful and they stop us dead in our tracks if we're reckless. We can't drive without the one, we can't natter without the other.

Insults and Put-Downs

Strictly speaking most of these prevent conversations, as we know them in the civilized sense, from even getting off the ground. But since I have always followed the maxim of returning like for like, civilization doesn't really enter into it. On the other hand, they can be very useful if you suddenly find yourself locked in verbal conflict with the sort of oafs most of us encounter from time to time, the sort who come up to one and say, 'I know that face. You're in that programme with Richard Briers, aren't you? I always have a laugh at that, you make such a twit of yourself, you remind me of myself sometimes. Who is it you play now?'

'The goat,' I answer.

I commented earlier on the unpleasantness with a taxi driver so it seems fair now to redress the balance with an example of how the rule of the road once got me off the hook after scoring maximum points.

This time I was in the line of traffic pottering along and minding my own business. Parked by the side of the road was a clapped-out old Ford Zodiac, which if my memory is right, was the pride of the Z Cars fleet when they first took to the streets of Newtown. I was studying the intricate pattern on its near-side wing which time, rust and a few half-hearted home repairs had clearly wrought, when to my amazement the heap limped out into the traffic right in front of me. As with the taxi-driver before, I slammed on my brakes and came to a halt a matter of inches from the transfer of the pussy-cat on the boot with the balloon coming out of its mouth saying, 'please keep off my tail'.

The driver behind had the wit to brake as well, so a pile-up was narrowly avoided, but I had to keep moving and this meant staying far closer to the car in front than I wanted to.

When we all ground to a standstill in a line of traffic about a mile later, the driver in front got out of his car and walked back to me looking like the wrath of God.

'Didn't you ever hear of the Highway Code?' he yelled at my window, 'Cos if you'd read it you'd know that you're driving too f***ing close. The safe stopping distance at 30 mph is at least 45 yards and you've been on my bumper all the time.'

'Didn't you read the bit about not doing anything that made another driver change direction or speed?' I asked, racking my brain to remember if that was correct, or if I had somehow got it muddled with what the Thames Conservancy man had said to me the day we nearly ran down a ludicrously flimsy boat with eight hearties flaying at the water near Kingston.

'Yeah, What of it?' asked my barrack-room lawyer.

'Well, in that case you'd realize that you'd made me do both of those when you pulled out . . . and if I'm not mistaken it also says somewhere that you're supposed to move when the lights turn green – which I'm doing and you're not, bye!'

Hearing someone deliver a really good put-down can be just as much fun. I reckon that we do pretty well in this country at the moment with the political fireworks which seem to shoot out of the Palace of Westminster every time someone lights the blue touch-paper before the house retires. I decided long before the American election, too, that part of the reason why the campaign never got the American nation excited was that the two contestants were so lacking in the essential qualities of wit and repartee which help to make politics tolerable to the ordinary chap. This hasn't always been the case, mind you. Two old chestnuts spring to mind which I never tire of hearing.

The first concerns one Al Smith addressing an election meeting when a heckler yelled out to him:

'Go on, Al, tell 'em all you know. It won't take long.' To which the politician replied instantly:

'If I tell all, we both know it won't take me any longer.'

The boot was on the other foot when Theodore Roosevelt was speaking at another election rally. A heckler interrupted him, yelling:

'What about me? I'm a Democrat.'

'May I ask you why you are a Democrat?' enquired Roosevelt.

'My grandfather was a Democrat, my father was a Democrat, so I'm a Democrat,' he shouted back.

'And may I therefore ask what do you suppose you would be if your grandfather had been a jackass and your father had been a jackass?'

'A Republican,' shouted the heckler triumphantly.

CONVERSATION STOPPERS №2

It looks for the time being as if wit of that type has buried its head in the sand in American politics at least, probably because it's the jackasses who now wield the power. But then they're probably the only ones who can be bothered with the responsibility and who are vain enough to think that it really matters. And this is even truer in the lower echelons of authority, from the man who tells you you can't wash your car in the road to the one who superintends the public loo in the park.

I always seem to have my greatest problems with people like this when I am in a hurry. Ticket collectors as a breed have that rare facility of getting me flustered just as the train is pulling away from the station. It doesn't matter how many times I might have reassuringly felt the ticket in my pocket on my way to the station, I can guarantee that as I pant towards the man checking the tickets, the wretched thing will escape and I'll have to go through the humiliation of turning out my pockets while fellow-passengers push past me in their frustration.

'We can't hold the train for you, sir,' the helpful railway staff tell me. 'You should have had your ticket ready if you knew you were going to be late.'

'I had it only a moment ago, in this pocket,' I try to explain, adding imploringly, 'Can I show it to the guard on the train when I've found it?'

'I'm afraid not, sir. It would be more than my life's worth to let you through without seeing your ticket.'

'I don't give a damn about your life, I've got to catch that train,' I then say, rapidly losing my sangfroid and starting to rummage through the contents of my suitcase.

'That sort of attitude isn't going to help you at all, sir,' says the ticket collector, his hackles rising. 'I don't suppose that would be the ticket in your breast pocket would it, sir?'

'Oh goodness, yes,' I'm forced to admit as I try to squeeze my pyjamas and sponge-bag back into the case without creasing my one clean shirt and without letting my slippers fall out of the side. 'Thank you so much. I must have stuck it in there for safe keeping and forgotten where I put it.'

'I expect you did, sir,' he tells me with a pitying smile. 'But I'm afraid you've come to the wrong platform. The train you want leaves in a couple of minutes from No. 11.'

So with further hurried apologies and muttered imprecations I gather my case, stick my ticket in my breast pocket and scuttle across the station to begin the whole beastly saga once again.

I hoped years ago, in my naïvety, that automation would make this sort of traveller's nightmare a thing of the past, but there again I was out of luck. Instead of the intransigent little man at the gate to the platform, the underground, at least, sports those fiendish little machines now which threaten, like eastern potentates, to emasculate anyone of average height who tries to pass through it and down the escalator.

'Put the ticket in the slot, mate,' the official told me once.

'Which ticket?' I asked in perfect innocence.

'Oh, Jesus,' said the man, 'You've got to get a ticket before you can go through the barrier.'

'Oh,' I said politely and joined the queue to buy my ticket, having no change to feed into a machine which threatened to send me to all points from Cockfosters to Whitechapel.

'Put the ticket in the slot, mate,' the man told me.

'Which slot?' I asked. There seemed to be any number to choose from.

'Oh, Jesus,' said the man. 'Not you again. The one marked Tickets.'

So I put my ticket into the slot, one half of the barrier flew open, I walked in and it slammed shut behind me.

'Don't forget your case,' the man said, just as I had negotiated the final pair of barriers.

I thought of getting back through the barrier but it was more than my life, or worse, was worth to hazard those snapping, black rubber jaws.

'I don't suppose you could pass it to me?' I asked the man.

'Oh, Jesus,' he said, and with insolent panache he picked up the case which I had barely been able to carry and vaulted over the barrier in one unruffled leap.

'Go on now, piss off,' he said. And I did, down the escalator to the wrong platform on the wrong line. I didn't have the nerve to go back up and ask if I could have a go at getting on to the right line, so I travelled under parts of London I had not visited since my youth and then spent a further ten minutes trying to explain to the inspector on the train why I was covering about four times the distance I should have covered. I travelled by taxi for several weeks after that.

I stopped buying papers in the rush hour for similar reasons. Something important had happened one day and when I saw a larger crowd than usual round the newspaper seller the herd instinct got to me and I found myself in the thick of the scrum.

'What's this?' the newspaper man asked when I handed him a fiver.

'The smallest change I have,' I told him, which as it happened was perfectly true.

'I don't believe it,' the man said bluntly. 'How am I supposed to give you change on the best news night of the year when they've given me an extra thousand copies to sell and the float's the same – and I've lost twenty sales already with you poncing about with your five pound notes.'

'Well, if you don't believe me, look at this,' I told him and for the only time in my life I took out a bunch of twenty pound notes which my wife wanted me to get to pay the builder who said he'd only do the job before Christmas if we paid cash.

'Blimey,' said the newspaperman, 'Sorry guv. You ain't anything to do with the paper are you, 'cos we've had these blokes round checking, you see.'

'I own it,' I told him, hastily grabbing my change and running down the steps to the station.

Of course it was a silly thing to say because I had to stop using that station for ages in case I met him again, and after the sudden triumph, embarrassment set in and I didn't buy another paper for months.

One of my brighter friends who went to university, instead of getting to grips with life, tells a good story about a fellow he knew while he was an undergraduate. This man was part of the governing body of the college and tended to let it go to his head, as most of them generally do. He was visiting London and riding on a bus when the conductor brushed past him rather rudely and then turned round to walk back down the aisle collecting the fares.

'Come on, mister, buck up your ideas, I've got the top deck to do yet and we haven't got all day.'

'I am the Dean of St John's,' the don told him haughtily, 'and I do not pay on London Transport.'

'Oh no, of course not, your grace,' said the conductor confused and thrown off his guard.

'But I still require my ticket, and I haven't got all day either,' said the don. And the conductor gave it free of charge, which just goes to show what a little nerve can do.

Another thing that I've stopped doing, though fortunately for

CONVERSATION STOPPERS (No 3)

other reasons, is going to launderettes. I always used to feel like some sort of voyeur anyway and the clothes never seemed to come out as clean as the ones washed in domestic washing machines.

I was in there once when a grubby old man came in with an even more revolting canvas bag, bursting at the seams with vile-smelling washing. He muttered something to the lady washing the floor and then went out again without attempting to put the clothes into a machine. It didn't take long for the warm, damp atmosphere of the launderette to take on the aroma of a cow-shed after milking. We all edged down the row of plastic chairs away from the offending bag and towards the door. The woman washing the floor quickly finished what she was doing and disappeared behind a hidden door in the plastic pine panelling.

The owner of the launderette then arrived after nipping across the road for a packet of fags and a drop of stout, and by now the stench had become virtually intolerable, but we were all ignoring it, as only the English can, each fixedly studying the circular glass door behind which our own washing was happily squelching and frothing away.

'Who in God's name left that there,' shouted the owner, giving the canvas bag a disdainful kick. 'Come on, whose is it? What filthy bastard's dumped this rotten load in here? It's yours, isn't it?' she yelled, singling out the timid little man reading *Autocar* at the end by the public telephone.

'No, mine's in here,' he said in a half-whisper.

'Not bloody likely,' said the good lady, somewhat confused by milk stout but still conscious of her role as proprietor. 'Get this load of stinking rags out of here now or I'll have the police round, so help me I will.'

'Ere Mrs Duckworth,' said the lady who'd been cleaning the floor. 'I've cleaned up out the back. We're out of Flash again and your old man popped in with that load of washing you wanted done. He put it down here somewhere.'

Moments like that are best savoured after some dreadful gaffe of one's own.

Authority in uniform can take on an even more menacing appearance, as I said before. It can make you look doubly a fool too, if you happen to have a face which is well known, like mine. Some years ago I had a brush with the law in which I suffered perhaps the greatest put-down of my career. By some quirk of justice I found that my car had been towed away from where I'd parked it. This was made even more frustrating by the fact that I had to get a taxi to take me to the police station where I could retrieve it. The taxi was punishment enough in those days, you literally had to go to the Building Society to get money out to pay for it. And then to pay £30 to get your car back was adding insult to injury.

But the final straw came after writing the cheque. The Superintendant then asked for my autograph. What else could I do but give it straightaway, but to make matters worse I also put down 'Good Luck, Richard Briers'. I ought to have known better!

I suppose that to give the complete picture of Briers vs. The Law

I ought to mention a similar episode which worked to my advantage. Never let it be said that I am anything but scrupulously fair when it comes to matters like this, though it has nothing whatsoever to do with being insulting. It did stop a conversation, however, and looking back it can be fairly said to have stopped a court appearance, too.

I was speeding at 40 mph when I was overhauled by one of those frightening policemen on motorcycles, who look as wide as they are heavy. I got out of my car – it seemed advisable – to apologize, knowing damn well that I was in the wrong.

'You know this is a 30 mile an hour limit?' he said.

'Yes. I'm terribly sorry,' I told him looking him straight in the eye. He looked me straight in the eye too and we stood there peering at each other by the side of the road as the world raced by. Then, after an electrifying pause like the one you sense when the chap's at the top of that awful ski-jump, he said:

'Well, one thing you can do for me.'

'What's that?' I asked, willing even to bump start his bike had he asked.

'Can you sign this for my daughter, please?'

And that was all there was to it.

Stunning Stoppers

There are those who can blind with science, but those who can't are advised, in my experience, to do the next best thing and amaze their listeners with bizarre gobbits of information, if necessary about any subject under the sun, but, ideally, connected with what they are talking about.

I have always been an addict for this kind of stuff. I've never given a damn if it's been true or not. What appeals is the sheer intellectual audacity of announcing boldly that the Deer Bot fly moves through the air faster than a rifle bullet, or that if you fired a rifle at Concorde travelling at top speed the plane would leave the bullet standing.

The lovely thing about dropping these mind-blowing pieces of information is that if you're lucky there's never anyone around sufficiently well read, or knowledgeable to question your judgement. And on the whole I've found that those that are sharp enough to see through what I've been saying are good enough sports not to let on openly. They enjoy the conceit as much as everyone else, and I wouldn't be surprised if some of them don't pepper their own conversation with the gems they glean from others, at a later date.

The obvious consequence of filling your mind with useless information and spewing it forth at any given opportunity is that you quickly become branded as a know-all. This can work to one's advantage, or disadvantage, depending on how it's handled.

I knew a terribly pretty girl who went out of her way to bore people to tears. She used this as a sort of acid test on everyone, and those who stuck around to listen to her rambling on from one amazing fact to another were the ones who got to know the sunnier side of her character.

I mean you've got to be pretty keen to take someone's hand, look into their eyes and then be told that more diseases are contracted by holding hands than by kissing, or that the cause of Henry VIII's syphilis was believed by many of his doctors to have been Cardinal Wolsey (or one of his crowd) whispering in the king's ear.

At the other end of the scale was the poor unfortunate who used to turn up to all the parties I went to when I was in my last years at school. At that age there always seemed to be the same faces at parties, only the venue and food changed, sometimes not even the latter. But this chap would swot up masses of stunning facts in the hope that someone would be fascinated by his erudition. But all that happened was that a group of the others would gang together and draw him out on one obscure line of thought that somehow always ended up with him disclosing the most intimate details about the animal kingdom; gestation periods of rhinoceroses; penis lengths of whales, bull elephants and harvest mice; coition records of apes studied in captivity and even more outrageous facts that time has obscured from my memory. He never made a huge success with girls because they were afraid that he would sooner or later blurt out some compromising information about them. The last I heard of him he was working in a library, where he was proving a great success.

But in spite of the fun at his expense I did take a leaf out of his book and started mugging up a few facts of my own which have been terribly useful at times when my brain has gone a complete blank. Although I say it myself the results have always been very gratifying, especially as the effort involved in picking up these sort of things is minimal, particularly if you earn your bread and butter by learning things, as I have to.

The only real criteria I stick to when it comes to drawing on my reserves of anything but general knowledge are that I should only seek to make an impression when more than one other person is present (not including a member of my family and close friends – who've heard them all before) and that when I am stuck for something to say the gobbit I choose should be as far removed from what I was previously talking about as to make its introduction almost as arresting as what is actually being said.

As for unearthing these bits and pieces, newspapers and biographies are fertile areas of research. For scientific stuff I have to rely on what my children tell me, so that side of things is a bit thin, not that they're poor informers, but simply because my own understanding of the physical sciences never progressed much beyond lighting the bunsen burner.

So on that note here are a couple of pages from my collection, one on the theatre, my pet subject, and one lot of miscellanea:

Theatre, Films and Movies

Did you know that:

Shaw wrote his last play *Farfetched Fables* when he was ninety-three, just one year before he died.

Sarah Bernhardt had a wooden leg towards the end of her career and often wore it on stage. She played Juliet when she was seventy. She often slept in a coffin lined with love letters (Note, after one unfortunate incident: check that no one in earshot has a false limb).

Anyone thinking of playing Hamlet uncut has to learn 11,610 words (Note: Shakespeare had red hair, could be a useful line with gorgeous red-heads. Be careful though, so did Winston Churchill).

At the beginning of the Second World War Hollywood was

turning out two films a day. Present-day Indian studios produce over one and a half a day. (When challenged to name one say you can't pronounce the name in Hindi and it loses everything in the translation.)

Before they cast Vivien Leigh as Scarlet O'Hara they spent over $90,000 and auditioned over 1,400 actresses for the part.

Sophocles wrote 123 plays but only 7 survive (Note: *Titus Andronicus* is *not* one of them).

Among the 30,000 extras in *Quo Vadis* there were 63 lions (Note: possible joke about these not being equity members but it not mattering as they didn't sing – *Archers* reference).

Pot Luck – or What You Will

Did you know that:

Bach wrote an opera about coffee.

You burn up as many calories making love as you do skipping.

Every planet in the Solar System could be placed inside Jupiter.

The ancient Romans used to eat dormice as a delicacy.

A medieval law in England made it illegal to keep Spanish wine and French wine in the same cellar.

The male spider has its penis on the end of one of its legs.

John I was king of France for four days.

Richelieu had a sister who thought her back was made from crystal and a brother who thought that he was God.

Dante wrote his first sonnet to Beatrice when he was nine.

Jane Russell's bosom was once the subject of four pages of notes written by Howard Hughes.

One of the leading pre-war French detectives was called Charles-Adolphe Faux-Pas Bidet.

Blunders and Bloomers

That last bit about the French detective makes a natural entry into the worst conversation stopper of them all, the accidental slip of the tongue that spells embarrassment and ruin.

There's nothing you can teach me about how to avoid putting my foot in it. I have now learned to tread more warily, to drink more moderately and to speak less frequently. So if you, too, have the unfortunate knack of turning the most innocent remark into an easily misunderstood insult my advice is to follow those three rules.

As a child I developed the habit of calling every older woman Auntie, no matter what her relationship to me was. All my friends' mothers were called Auntie Mary, Auntie Anne or Auntie Liz. But the grandest of these was Auntie Cynthia, who never took to my winning, childish personality and who seemed to be slightly unsure of my mother as well.

Auntie Cynthia was George's mum, but I didn't have much time for George, which might explain some of her antipathy towards me. They lived in rather grander style than we did and Auntie Cynthia was always dressed in a way that was calculated to set her above everyone else's mum. Today they would be called nouveau riche. When I was little they were just plain stuck-up.

George's birthday was between Christmas and New Year, so he always had a party that combined all the other celebrations.

The year in question was the one when George's mum had been given a dazzling new outfit for Christmas by George's dad. The ensemble would have been ideally suited to a diplomatic reception on a warm tropical night. But for a children's party scheduled for 3 o'clock on a dank December afternoon, it was faintly absurd, to put it mildly.

Auntie Cynthia was so thrilled with her latest present, however, that she bravely faced the icy afternoon gusts at the front door like one of the Valkyries, swathed in yards of eddying chiffon, welcoming us all to Valhalla.

My mother had never been inside the house, on a point of principle, but she was asked in for a cup of tea when she came to collect me, and there was little she could do but accept.

The children's side of the party broke up after a final game of hunt-the-thimble which ended in an unseemly brawl when George accused one of his guests (not me, of course) of cheating. We all spilled into the drawing-room, as Auntie Cynthia insisted on calling it, where our mothers were sitting uncomfortably making small talk.

I can remember to this day going up to my mother, who was telling Auntie Cynthia how nice the Christmas tree looked and how nice it was to see real candles on the tree, feeling flushed and excited. Auntie Cynthia was handing round delicate little sandwiches on a pretty plate covered with a doily. 'Would you like one, Dicky?' she asked me bending right down to offer me one.

I took three.

'Isn't this a lovely house, dear?' my mother asked loudly, hoping that I would say something flattering while George's mother was still in earshot.

'Smashing,' I said, with two-thirds of my haul shoved into my mouth. 'It's so big inside. The door's like a castle door. But Mummy, did you see Auntie Cynthia's knockers. I nearly grabbed one, but I couldn't quite reach it. Why don't you have ones like that?'

It's curious how penetrating a child's voice can be, especially when all other conversation dies away.

I thought I was going to get a real hiding when we got home, to judge by what my mother said in George's house, but she seemed quite pleased with me afterwards.

I got off less lightly in later encounters. A shop counter was the scene of one of my more unforgivable blunders. Again it was approaching Christmas and there were crowds of people to witness my folly. I was buying some presents in Foyles with a Book Token I had been given the year before and was using up before its time ran out. For some reason I was in a better than average mood at that time of the year. Perhaps a cheque had turned up, for something had put me into a rosy state of mind that made me forgive the hordes of rude, shoving people surging from counter to cashier and back again.

I wanted to ask the assistant to look something up for me when I went to collect my books and seeing that there were lots of people waiting to collect their books, I gave a knowing smile to let her know I would forsake my place in the queue to help her clear the backlog of customers.

The smile she gave me back put me into an even better frame of mind.

I only had to wait a couple of miutes and I was on the point of asking her to get out *Books in Print* for me when a grey-haired customer came bustling up, obviously in a great hurry.

'It's all right,' I said engagingly, 'Do serve this gentleman first.'

The man didn't move forward, so I took his arm saying, 'Please go ahead sir, I don't mind waiting.'

The iron-grey head turned and the face gave me a thin smile through pale lipstick and face-powder.

Even the assistant at the counter was looking daggers at me and my seasonal air thoroughly evaporated.

My clever chum, the one I mentioned earlier who had been to Oxford, took a perverse delight in rowing. I don't think he was ever much good at it, but he enjoyed the après-row, or whatever they call it when they crawl through the watery slime back into the club house and emerge an hour or so later dry on the outside but soaked on the inside. He met some very interesting types during his time at Oxford and the rowing club always seemed a convenient haven for foreigners, particularly for refugees from behind the Iron Curtain.

One of the most colourful of these was a Hungarian who made it hot-foot from Budapest in 1956 after lobbing a handful of rocks at

ONE SIDED CONVERSATIONS (No2)

SURGERY

a Russian tank. The story of this fellow's escape is fascinating enough and would legitimately stop any conversation. But that isn't the point of this anecdote. He had been a rower (or oarsman, as rowers like to call themselves) before his flight and as he'd been quite good he had met a number of English rowers at regattas on the continent. So it was only natural that, when he arrived in London destitute and almost without knowing a word of the language, he should have fallen in with them and their cronies.

No one was ever quite sure what he did by way of a living, but as time went by he started to get some very impressive invitations to formal receptions and diplomatic parties. Rumours were rife that he was some sort of escaped royalty, or a spy, or both. But he used his limited English as a front to parry any searching questions.

Anyhow my chum's story goes that at one of these early do's

this fellow turned up in white tie and behaved impeccably all evening in spite of the fact that his only friends in London at that time were the raucous, if well-meaning, argonauts of the Tideway. When the time came for him to leave he presented himself to his hostess, gallantly kissed her gloved hand and with a beaming smile thanked her in rather florid terms for a delightful evening.

She was so charmed by his behaviour that she tried to persuade him to stay a little longer, which seemed to throw him off his guard and his previous command of 'the English' went out of the window.

'That would be very nice, my lady. But for me it will not be so. It is time now I bugger off.'

And he did without further delay when the smiling faces around him registered their astonishment.

There are a fortunate few who seem to be able to sail confidently through situations like this and come out quite unruffled. The young mother in the train is a case in point. To begin with, anyone who has the 'cool' to breast-feed a baby in public, in this country at least, isn't easily put out by a mere slip of the tongue. This girl wasn't one of the last swallows of the hippy summer, though. She was elegantly clothed and read *Cosmopolitan*, which, come to think of it, might have explained her behaviour.

The train was somewhere between Swindon and Bristol when she calmly unbuttoned her blouse and offered her offspring lunch. The baby had other ideas, however. It had probably noticed that the bar was open and that other passengers were hastily downing their first drink in order to squeeze in a second before the train ploughed into Bristol Temple Meads at its breathtaking hundred miles an hour.

Mother tried to coax it for several minutes, but it kept turning its head aside and finally started to wail.

'Well, if you don't want it,' she said, 'I'll give it to the man opposite.'

The poor chap, who was already having the devil of a time trying to concentrate on the interior of his briefcase and drink at the same time, spurted gin and tonic all over the minutes he was reading.

'Oh, I am sorry,' said the girl, quite unabashed, 'Dryden's being so difficult this morning. Do let me buy you another drink, and if I give you the money could you get one for me, too. At least one of us will get what's good for them.'

Of course it can be argued that the lady in question didn't actually interrupt any conversation of her own by that remark, but I'm damn sure she silenced everyone else in the carriage.

There is another breed of remark which doesn't so much stop a conversation because it comes out accidentally but because of what has been said and the way it's been said.

The best examples I can think of happen to come from Americans and perhaps this is an indication of the cultural and social gap that still divides us from the New World.

Years ago I was appearing in a Noel Coward play, which had got some fairly good notices and was drawing good houses. One night an elderly American, who must have been at least thirty years older than me, came round the back to see me. I was feeling bright and chatty and asked him into the dressing room, but he only stood in the doorway and said, 'Sir, may I say how much I have always reverenced your art.' There's not a lot you can say to that.

Other examples come from an amazing hostess in one of the smarter areas of New England. I've never met this lady, but her reputation is legendary among British artists. Her whole manner apparently gives the impression that she's trying to intimidate her visitors, when really she's only trying to put them at their ease. It's just that her remarks do not lubricate the easy flow of conversation so much as give it a shot of high-octane additive. She has been known to offer around cigarettes with the nonchalant remark, 'Cancer anyone?' And at one celebrated meal she offered one of her more diffident guests a second helping which was being persistently refused with the final encouragement, 'Come on, you can eat it now and vomit later.'

Bolt-Holes or Sudden Exits

There comes a time in the life of most ordinary people when they find themselves at a loss for words. Sometimes they are overcome with joy, which is nice. Sometimes they are overcome with grief, which is tragic and demands sympathy. But sometimes, as is far more likely to be the case, they are overcome with the dreadful realization that they have dropped the most frightful brick, which no amount of explaining can excuse.

When this happens and you're left gaping and astonished at your own stupidity there is only one sensible thing to do – run like hell.

Common courtesy still has a part to play in an orderly retreat, however, and unless you can guarantee going into a dead faint at a moment's notice, it's much safer to have a few good excuses up your sleeve to get you out of harm's way as quickly as possible.

My wife has a splendid stock of domestic crises which she calls on at any time of the day and in any situation. Something left in the oven, the bath left running (only for telephone calls or people calling at the front door), the children to fetch from somewhere, the sweep/plumber/builder/decorator calling to do some urgent work on the house – all these can be brought into play when and if the need arises.

I'm rather less fortunate myself in this respect and on the whole my only convincing line of escape is the dog. Dogs are man's best friends in more than mere companionship. A humble spaniel can be just as much of a life-saver, when you're out for a walk and put your foot in it, as the St Bernard with its little barrel of brandy halfway up a mountain.

I don't take a lot of interest in politics, especially local politics, so I never know the names of people standing for the council elections, and this is my excuse for my embarrassment with our local Liberal candidate, who approached me as I was taking Paddy for a walk to do his number ones and twos. He introduced himself and seemed a pleasant enough sort of a chap, and as neither of the

other candidates had been round even to pass the time of day with me, I thought it would be courteous to chat to him. We were actually getting on rather well and I said to him, 'At least you're not cursed with the awful wife that last poor sod had. I'm not surprised he left her in the end, she virtually ruined his chances of getting elected and from what I heard her ideas of being liberal amounted to offering her favours to any Tom, Dick, or Harry who took her fancy. The last thing I heard was that she'd taken up with some little twerp who fancied himself as the next Jeremy Thorpe.'

I was about to launch forth on another salacious gem that I'd picked up from the local grapevine when we were joined by a woman who'd been popping in and out of houses along the street delivering leaflets.

The candidate introduced us a little formally I thought.

'Pleased to meet you', said his wife. 'Didn't my ex know you?

He was the last Liberal candidate for this ward. You must remember him?'

'Paddy!' I screamed and went charging down the road to fetch him from the verge where he was lying quietly under a tree, trying to distance himself from my histrionics.

I didn't vote that year, it didn't seem right.

I found that measures like this tend to be needed more for getting out of conversations with people you don't want to talk to at all; people like the bank manager, the chairman of the Residents Action Committee, and the man who is so boring that no one else is talking to him. Into this category I also group those functions which I'm forced to attend without really wanting to.

Oscar Wilde invented Bunburying, and Ellen Terry had her little illnesses. I've taken a leaf out of her book. If I know that any engagement is going to be too awful to bear, I succumb to whatever's going around at the time.

Some people who can't avoid these functions think up terribly elaborate schemes to get away early. I know one chap who gets a friend to telephone him half an hour after the do is due to start to call him away on urgent business, which can be anything from the arrest of one of his children to a sudden flurry of activity on the Tokyo Stock Exchange.

Another friend never goes anywhere without a hypodermic syringe and a small glass phial in his pocket. If he feels boredom or trouble looming on the horizon all he has to do is to reach into his pocket and produce his two props saying something like, 'Good heavens, is that the time. I'm half an hour late. Would you please excuse me while I go to the bathroom and give myself a shot of this.' The phial only contains water and anyone who knows anything about syringes would see that his was obsolete years ago. It's the bluff that counts.

I've heard of people pretending to have epileptic fits, of others deliberately smashing glasses in pubs to cause diversions, but the simplest and by far the most authentic means of escape is the call of nature. The sudden, pressing need for a pee has saved me more times than I care to remember. No one wants you to hang around a moment longer than you need once you've mentioned the subject, and providing your reason for getting away is not because you've committed a frightful blunder, no one should take offence at your hasty departure.

But hopefully, the need for desperate measures like these will diminish with a greater understanding of the drift of any conversation. If we pick up alarm signals early on we can save ourselves no end of struggling when we get into hot water, by simply not plunging in in the first place.

That's why being able to read and write between the lines, metaphorically speaking, is such an important part of conversation.

6

E*h*?

understanding conversation

If, like me, you were brought up to believe that conversation was a means of communicating, in other words of getting your ideas across to the next chap simply and clearly, then, like me, you must have had a rude shock when you first realized that what was being said didn't always go hand in hand with what was meant. Interpreting conversation is very much an art of its own.

I first discovered this when I was about ten. I couldn't understand why my parents had never taken up the offer of spending a weekend with some frightfully smart people we'd met on holiday a year or two before. They'd told us about their home in the country and their dozen horses and in my innocence it sounded an invitation not to be refused.

So it came as a grave disappointment when my mother explained that there was the world of difference between an invitation that was given as, 'You really must come and spend a weekend with us when you're down our way sometime,' and one given in these terms, 'You really must come and spend next weekend with us.'

In such cases as much subtlety is called for on the part of the speaker as on that of the listener. There's no earthly point in saying to someone, 'It's very close today, isn't it, would you mind if I opened the window just a little?', to have him reply, 'Oh, sorry mate, I didn't think you'd notice. It must have been the shepherd's

117

pie.' It's really a form of verbal shorthand that we use to gloss over things that we prefer not to have to say openly.

There are some people who are actually paid for doing this. I'm thinking in particular of press attachés and other official spokesmen, like the American air force officer in Cambodia, who told the world's press after one notorious US bombing raid, 'You always write it's bombing, bombing, bombing. It's not bombing, It's air support.'

Others in positions of lesser authority can be just as good, though. A few years ago I read about a Pakistani who was refused permission to join a club somewhere. The press got on to it and so did the race relations people. But the club secretary came out with the priceless comment to one reporter, 'We didn't turn down his application. We just didn't accept it.'

Distasteful as this is to the purists, and to those young enough not to appreciate its value, there's little doubt that conversation as we understand it would fold up if the art of the innuendo and the euphemism suddenly disappeared. Half the fun of dropping subtle hints and reading between the lines would go as well, along with the delight of sharing racy gossip in otherwise respectable surroundings.

One of the lessons that's come home to me over the years is that it's no good being merely able to disguise my meaning. I have had to learn how to pick up other people's meanings. It is all part of avoiding the sort of terrible predicaments that I've mentioned earlier.

As an actor I've always been terribly conscious of the hidden meaning behind what people say to me, particularly in relation to my work. For this reason I am wary of the slightly camp directors who phone me up from time to time with unprepossessing offers of work like this:

'I can't tell you much about it now, lovie. But we know you'll adore it. It's been written by this terribly exciting young Puerto Rican who's gone down very big in Latin America. I know it's a bit out of your line, but I think it'll be very good for you, I really do. We

all feel it will stretch you and this is terribly important at your time of life and at this stage in your career.'

Experience has taught me that suggestions like this usually entail trooping out to Tooting or somewhere else in the suburbs to spend the evening in a smoke-filled annexe of a seedy pub, either taking off all my clothes or being lashed to a kitchen chair and moaning for a couple of hours, all for £8 a week plus the tube fare and a free pint of Watneys.

Auditions can be harrowing experiences, too, particularly if you're just getting going and are having a few of the rough edges knocked off. Some directors can be absolute brutes. I've known one tell a really quite presentable actress, 'I only cast pretty girls.' And there was another horror who used to make young actors do the most humiliating things just for the fun of it. 'Right, I'd like you to pretend you're an exploding caterpillar,' was one of his favourite lines, and that was for a production of *Uncle Vanya*.

Most of them are rather more subtle in what they say, and contrary to what we're always told, I've never heard anyone say,

'Don't ring us we'll ring you.' The more common line of approach is, 'Thank you. That was very nice. You've certainly great power of expression and we particularly liked that bit of impromptu business when you caught your foot in the trap as you came on. Of course there are several others waiting to audition and we can't give you a positive answer now. But an idea did occur to us as you were reciting that last soliloquy. Have you ever thought of Theatre in Education? It's a tremendous challenge of course, and as it happens a colleague of mine in Truro is on the lookout for a replacement – I mean another actor to join his rapidly growing team. Would you like me to give you his phone number, just in case?'

Then of course there are the shop assistants, usually in the smarter shops I've found, who try to steer you into buying something that you had no intention of buying in the first place. They try on lines like, 'I do think that suits you, sir. It has a dignity about it which is far and away superior to that' (pointing to the new suit you really prefer and which is £80 cheaper).

And there are the other sort who take one look at you when you tell them the size you want and suggest, 'Perhaps sir would care to try on this to begin with. Being continental you'll find that it's cut rather differently, but I think that'll fit sir very well. And it's always best to allow a little room in case anything goes on underneath.' The customer is left to flatter himself that the man's probably referring to a waistcoat or a vest. Of course he's talking about a different sort of insulation.

The most difficult time to pick up these signals, however, is when one's half-cut. The trouble is that it's then that they're most likely to be sent out. Wives are a tower of strength at this time. They keep dropping increasingly less subtle hints, while the men natter on and make fools of themselves, until they finally have to give us a kick on the shin and lead us away saying something about a gammy leg.

But they can be a hazard when they stumble on one's minor social indiscretions. I love the story of the wife who decided to meet her husband at the Squash Club and got into conversation with a girl who blithely told her that he'd been giving her 'a few lessons'.

'How interesting,' said the wife, 'I'm very pleased to meet you. Geoffrey's told me so little about you.'

Then there's the wonderful way that women can put each other down without sounding nearly as offensive as they are being. The incident at the Squash Club reminds me of a celebrated remark overheard at the local tennis club after a mixed doubles game one Sunday afternoon.

'That was a super game, Mandy,' said one wife to the other. 'Nigel and I thought that you and Adrian put up a very spirited resistance in that last set. It was such a shame that Adrian's service let him down early on in the match.'

'Thank you,' said the other wife, 'I'm so pleased you won, though – I doubt if I could have borne another scene like the last time.'

But I think the subtlest remark I've ever heard was one given by the wife of a friend of mine to the very flighty, but rather dim wife of an antique dealer she knew quite well.

'Of course the trouble with you, my dear,' said my friend's wife, 'is that you're married to a cuckold.' To which the antique dealer's wife replied with great interest, 'Do you really think so?'

When it comes to disguising my own conversation however, I rather fancy myself as a diplomatist, a skill which hasn't come through any lack of practice. Whether it's been a case of having suddenly to think of something to say when I've been put on the spot by dreadful relatives threatening a visit, or whether I've found myself having to say something flattering about a terrible meal, I've always been fortunate to dredge up something plausible from the recesses of my mind.

Unfortunately, in the case of the badly-cooked meal, whatever excuse I've used, I've never got away without eating at least some of the food. I usually put the blame onto myself by saying, 'How clever of you to produce tripe. I haven't eaten it for ages, but you'll have to forgive me if I only indulge myself moderately, because, like a fool, I got talked into having rather a big lunch.'

Another good approach, which I have never used, but which I hear works just as well, is the one about the diet. 'It's a damn good thing you didn't invite us last night' (to one's hostess), 'because I might not be here now to enjoy this. I had a bit of a shock this morning when I went for the life insurance check-up. The doctor told me to lose at least a stone before the end of the year – said it would be the chop if I didn't. So, hard as it is, I'm afraid I'll have to stick to the greens. Good thing he didn't say anything about the vino, eh!'

One line that I take when I'm invited out to lunch and the food's awful is to eat some of it with apparent enjoyment and then put down my knife and fork as if to have a rest and say, 'I love this kind of food because it's so filling.' That permits me to leave at least a good half, but it also leaves open the option of stoking up with cheese or pudding if, as I desperately cross my fingers, they turn out to be better.

I find it most difficult to say something polite to friends when they put me on a spot and force me to say something relatively honest. The question of appearance is a difficult one in this situation, particularly when it comes to commenting on weight.

I know most of my friends well enough to tell them to their face what I think about their clothes. But it's not so easy when I'm confronted by one who's suddenly blown out like a balloon, which seems to be happening with alarming frequency at the moment. I think the best thing to do is to comment on it straightaway. He knows as well as I do that he's a good stone heavier than when I last saw him, so there's no point in trying to kid him that he hasn't changed shape. So I usually say how well he looks, make some reference to how drawn he looked last time and tell him how much the extra pounds suit him. Then I drop the topic for a few minutes to come back with a punch line a little later, along the lines that on consideration he definitely looks much more attractive. I like to think that this shows that I'm not in any way embarrassed by

chatting to a baby elephant and that I'm obviously thinking sympathetically about the change that's come over him.

What I've had to learn to avoid doing is a sudden U-turn when he's told me that he really feels like a pig and wants to get down to his former weight as quickly as he can. You can't suddenly change course and say, 'Of course you're quite right, you really ought to think about a diet, particularly at your time of life. It can't be doing your poor old heart any good,' immediately after giving him the line about never having looked so well in his life. It doesn't sound sincere. On the whole, its easier to cover your tracks with people you *don't* regard as bosom pals. One of the first problems is what to say when you've forgotten their names. Actors are often criticized for their habit of calling everyone 'darling', but bearing in mind the number of people they meet, it's about the only sure way, in their minds, of not giving offence.

There are various ways of covering up that you've forgotten someone's name. You can try to find out what it is by asking questions like, 'How did you say you spell your name?', though you might find yourself landed with the smart-alec who answers, 'S-for staphyloma, M-for mithridatism, I-for infundibulum, T-for trypanosoma and H-for hemiplegia.' On the other hand you can try to brazen it out by openly admitting, 'How can I possibly be expected to concentrate on a name when I see a face like this for the first time? Now, tell me again, what it is, now that I can apply my mind to putting the two together.'

Assuming that you survive this first encounter and you don't find them frantically interesting there's always the risk that you might be forced into issuing them an invitation, when it's really the last thing you want to do.

Again, having a dog comes in handy. I usually phrase the invitation with Paddy very much to the fore, in the hope that not everyone likes dogs as much as we do. 'We'll always be glad to see you,' I say as cheerfully as I can, 'Don't believe what people tell you about the labrador, he's as good as gold, as long as you don't put his back up. It's the essential frustration of all gun-dogs. They've got the hunter instinct, but they've been trained to fetch and carry for so long that they've got all mixed-up inside. Ours is fine though, with grown-ups. But I don't think it would be a good idea to bring the kids – not just at the moment anyway. Still I hope I haven't put you off dogs, ours always make quite an impression on our visitors, as I'm sure you'll find.'

Then I pop back with a fiendish final word, 'By the way don't wear anything too smart, will you? Ann does her best, but it's a losing battle with Paddy's hairs and the central heating. He keeps moulting all year round and you can't get them off some materials for love or money. Anyway I just thought I'd warn you. See you soon!'

Putting people off their nasty habits, like smoking, can be a bit tricky as well, if it's done without causing offence.

'You don't mind if I have a fag?' asks the smoker, 'I haven't had one since lunch and I'm desperate.'

'Go ahead,' says the non-smoker, with just a hint of regret in his voice. 'I wish I could join you but you've got to listen to what they tell you, haven't you. And I'd no idea I was that bad until the doctor showed me the X-ray of my insides. Of course I don't really understand all that he was saying, but it fair turned me over I can tell you, all that black sludge, it was like the bottom of a cess-pit. And then when I saw those other poor bleeders on the telly, you know, the ones who had their legs drop off because they'd been smoking sixty a day for forty years, well that was enough. I could see the writing on the wall, quite apart from the writing on the side of the packet, if you take my meaning. Still, don't let me put you off. You enjoy it while you can, that's what I say.'

Giving people references can be a tricky business at times, or so I'm told. Luckily I've never had to do it myself, which is just as well because I'd be hopeless if somebody came up to me and asked casually, 'We've been approached by that chap Halliday in your export department about a job we've got in Ulan Bator. Strictly off the record what's he like, Dicky?' Especially if I knew that the chap was an out-and-out rotter and nothing would be better than to see him packed off to some non-colonial extremity.

However, others with a greater facility and a quicker mind for this sort of thing can come up with an off-the-cuff reply which covers a multitude of sins. They say things like, 'Well, between you and me, if you can get him to work for you, you'll certainly be very fortunate,' or, if the chap in question is as thick as two short planks and they can't wait to off-load him onto some other firm, they'll say, 'Naturally, I'm biased, but it wouldn't be fair not to admit that he's a trier. He'll give you all he's got. He won't keep anything back. I think he'll go down a bomb with the yaks!' And that's all part of being able to use the right words at the right time, to interpret the conversation of being able to get onto the other chap's wavelength in fact.

Now anyone with a grain of sense can hardly have failed to notice that there is a worrying trend developing in everyday speech – the trend to circumlocute, confuse, elaborate and gener-ally muck about with perfectly acceptable words, titles, phrases and expressions with the sole purpose of making them sound more important and authoritative.

I'm dead against this. For one thing it's totally unnecessary and, for another, I can't understand the half of it, which is hardly surprising when a simple chat, which after all this book is about, becomes 'a relatively unstructured conversational situation'.

Much as I abhor this state of affairs, however, let no one call me an old stick-in-the-mud. I can move with the times as well as the next man, and so I swallow my pride and the words I would choose to use, and come out instead with the sort of self-conscious verbiage that we usually associate with the executive of the NUS and teachers of sociology.

Mind you I only resort to this when I am in 'a conversational situation' that demands language of this type – trying, for instance, to remonstrate with employees of the local council, from the Assistant Treasurer down to the chap who empties the litter bins, or when confronted with a visitor from the Inland Revenue, which mercifully happens once in a blue moon.

Before launching into one of these sessions I usually prime myself on the words I should use to give my conversation the stamp of up-to-the-minute acceptability and (what it's intended to give, after all), that definitive ring of polysyllabic incomprehensibility.

These are some of the favourites I've jotted down in my notebook, with their real meanings:

Jargon	Briers
Correctional therapeutic community	Prison
Preponderance	Greater weight
Antecedent to	Before
Money motivated	Greedy
Negative deficit	Profit
Totality of circumstances	Whole picture
Glass maintenance operative	Window cleaner
In the vicinity of	Near

Earned compensation	Pay
Landscape technician	Gardener
Socially disadvantaged underachiever	Poor, backward person
Low-cost	Cheap
Manipulative methods	Bribery
Conjecture, speculate	Guess
Substantially contemporaneous	About the same time
Aggregate of, totality of	All
To have an alcohol problem	To drink
Word processing unit	Typing pool
Information retrieval administrator	Filing clerk
Tonsorial artist	Hairdresser
Clinic for the emotionally disadvantaged	Loony bin
Multimedia systems technician	Film projectionist
Relocate	Move
Acquiesce, concur	Agree
Revenue agent	Tax collector
Converse	Talk
Perceptible, visible	In sight
Canine control officer	Dog catcher
Sanitation maintenance superintendent	Janitor

This frightening list leads naturally to the equally frightening topic of understanding jargon in conversation and learning how to converse, sorry, talk with any jargoneer on his own level.

Jargon – Retrieval, Assimilation and Utilization Situation

I'm convinced that half the reason why people don't get on with each other has nothing to do with their inability to speak the same language, in the sense that one can't make head nor tail of what the other's saying because he's foreign. No, the problem arises from their mistaken belief that they can understand each other because they use words in the English language. Only when it's too late does it dawn on one of them, if not on both, that the meanings they attach to these words and the context in which they are used are quite different. Though as I've discovered, and I'm sure most other people have, too, the situation is complicated by a lot of people using words which the ordinary chap has never heard before in his life.

It's all a question of culture.

Now, I can't speak a word of French and I certainly can't speak any of those odd Scandinavian languages, but this has never stopped me from getting on far better with people who come from north of John O'Groats than those who live south of Dover.

Scandinavians don't eat horse flesh for one thing and they don't try to shove their awful cultural smugness down your throat every time you mention Macaulay, Elgar or Constable. So, in a nutshell, I find it far easier to tune into the Nordic races than into the Gallo-Latin axis, because we operate on a similar wavelength.

However, talking to foreigners is really the least of my conversational worries when I think of the difficulty I have in understanding what some of my fellow Anglo-Saxons are saying. This has nothing to do with accent or dialect. It's brought about entirely by the vernacular or jargon that they insist on using.

I reckon this is used quite a lot of the time to cover up what is really being said. It's as if they carry on their whole dialogue in the small print at the bottom of the page instead of the bold headlines writ large at the top. And there are occasions when they don't even *realize* that their vernacular is going straight over my head.

I mean what is the man in the street supposed to make of a comment like this, when he asks his child's prospective headmaster, 'How's the timetable organized?':

'Over the past ten years the school has evolved a child-centred individual-learning situation with a degree of integrated day organization and close co-operation between each year's mixed-ability classes. Basic work morning programmes are carefully structured but allow for integration.'

Not that I am totally free from blame myself, for an actor often slips into his own jargon, the language of the theatre. There have been occasions when, in my nervous excitement, I have held forth with a series of theatrical anecdotes muttering things about people

'dropping irons' and omitting to point out to my listeners that I was referring to a blunder by the stage-manager in lowering the safety-curtain accidentally, and not to any calamity in the wardrobe.

Things got even more confusing when I really got carried away and told stories about stage-hands letting things drop from the 'flies, down between the legs to see if it would frighten the chorus girls to come on too early'. I got off pretty lightly, though, with nothing more than a few reproachful looks.

There are in fact jargons for every walk of life and every occupation. I've already commented on the bank manager and that race of financial wizards, set apart from *homo sapiens*, the ones who complain vehemently about the cost of living and yet who manage to get away with paying next to no income tax and qualifying for full local authority grants when they decide to redo the en-suite bathroom with raw silk on the walls and gold-plated taps (the one is insulation, the other non-corrosive plumbing materials).

But there are jargons, too, for schoolchildren, disc jockeys, the underworld, sportsmen, the women in Fine Fare and the media, to mention but a few. Most of these, though, fall into the category of that splendid French word 'argot', which refers to what we would call 'slang' and not, as I was once misinformed, to 'a snail before it has been cooked'.

No, the jargons to which I take exception and the ones that we should really try to master, if only to call the jargoneers' bluff, are those that are quite obviously élitist and exclusive, the ones which are deliberately contrived to set the jargoneer apart from the person he's talking to and establish a sort of social and intellectual one-upmanship. These are the ones which intimidate us and which are so often used to draw the wool over our eyes.

There are people who would honestly prefer to tell you it is raining by saying, 'there is a significant proportion of precipitation in the atmosphere'. These are the same people who, on finding that they've missed winning £50,000 on Ernie by one lousy digit, will throw their hands up and mutter phlegmatically, 'This is consistent with the vicissitudes of the sublunary experience in which we find ourselves,' instead of pouring a large Scotch and saying, 'Such is life'. And they're the ones who lack the imagination to appreciate that proverbs are not improved by replacing 'A nod's as good as a wink to a blind horse', with the observation, 'A minor inclination of the cranium is as adequate as a spasmodic movement of one optic to an equine quadruped utterly devoid of any visionary capacity.'

It's true to say of course that not many of us come face to face with the worst offenders, but we do have to listen to them being interviewed on the radio and the television, which is even more worrying in some ways because so often they are presented to us as experts.

Here's one of them commenting on an industrial job evaluation scheme, which is a bit of a mouthful in itself: '. . . there are grounds for thinking that the availability of analytical assessments of jobs would facilitate the preparation of grade-descriptions for a new structure in a situation in which the allocation of jobs to grades at the stage of implementing and maintaining that structure would be undertaken by whole-job procedure.'

I suppose it's possible that there was someone concerned with the scheme who could understand what the chap was saying, but I doubt if he got much feed-back from the shop floor. I would also put good money against any of the members of one school's PTA having the remotest idea of what this headmaster was saying when he told them about a new teaching policy which was being forced onto their offspring:

'Our school's cross-graded, multi-ethnic, individualized learning programme is designed to enhance the concept of an open-ended learning programme with emphasis on a continuum of multi-ethnic academically enriched learning using the identified intellectually gifted child as the agent or director of his own learning. Major emphasis is on cross-graded, multi-ethnic learning with the main objective being to learn respect for the uniqueness of a person.'

It's curious how often teachers seem to resort to this sort of language. I'm sure it's because they see themselves as the champions of sociology at the grass roots.

Now I've nothing against sociology as a discipline, well, not much anyway, but where I draw the line is the point when sociologists and their disciples start to litter their conversation with words that I don't, won't or can't understand and which I hear bandied about by any number of self-appointed know-alls or woolly-minded intellectuals who can't express themselves simply and concisely.

I'm quite prepared to admit that when a sociologist uses these words, he or she does so because they are technical words that form part of their academic discipline. The trouble is that so much of their vocabulary comes out of the wrong mouths that it gets terribly muddled and loses its original scientific meaning.

So, as far as I'm concerned, they're all tarred with the same brush.

These are my pet hates:

Defunctionalized	Ameliorating
Substantive	Constructivism
Periodicity	Synchronous
Falsificatory	Positivistic
Appropriative	Systematized
Extrapolation	Contributory
Usurpative	Deteriorative
Concordant	Interdependence
Transfigurative	Nonfragmenting
Exemplificatory	Interfractional
Factionalism	Discontinuity
Exponential	Inductive
Diversifying	Self-validating
Determinative	Aggregating
Eventuality	Synthesis
Eliminative	Solidification
Psychosis	Predicative

I need to have my back to the wall before I start padding out my conversation with anything like that. I can't pronounce half of them anyway.

But where I do try to make an effort to learn the everyday vocabulary of other people's jargon is in the slang they use. Calling a carpenter a 'chippy' when you, or your wife, is negotiating with a builder shows that you might have some idea of the difference between a barge board and a purlin, even if you're convinced that one refers to canal craft and the other to knitting.

To my way of thinking the remark made by Carl Sandburg in *The New York Times* that, 'slang is a language that rolls up its

sleeves, spits on its hands and goes to work', sums up its value. It shows people that you mean business. It shows them, too, that you're sufficiently interested in them to talk to them in terms with which they can easily identify. It may sound patronizing, but it's a good deal more effective in getting on with strangers than refusing to talk to them at all on the grounds that you can't get through to each other.

The only major thing I've had to watch when using slang is that I don't come out with words that are obsolete. Nothing's worse than making an idiot of yourself by chatting away happily in yesterday's language. This doesn't happen very often, but I've learned to watch what I say when I'm talking to my children's friends and others from that age group, where a wrong 'man' or 'groovy' could make me the laughing stock of the neighbourhood and send me to Coventry for a week.

When I'm in doubt I tend to play safe and make no attempt to introduce any slang into my conversation until I'm about to leave.

Then I'll look at my watch and say, 'It's been nice talking to you. Perhaps we'll meet again. But now it's time I hit the trail/split/drag out/take a powder/beat it/cut out,' followed by a chuckle which I hope covers any possible anachronism with a wry dig at myself. Then I disappear hastily, leaving my companion to ask, 'Say, who was that guy?'

'Don't you know?' someone will answer, 'That's the Lone Ranger.'

Well, something like that, anyway.

Glancing down one of my pages of up-to-the-minute, cool, 'rap' I notice that it's already getting a bit long in the tooth. But used with caution and in company that isn't too discerning it can be useful; and it also acts as an *aide memoire* of things not to say when I next get interviewed on Radio 1, or the *Old Grey Whistle Test*.

Most of these were jotted down on beer mats, or the back of bus tickets, as soon as I heard them, so they went into the book in any old order, which is how they come out here:

Far out	Incredible, very exciting
Uptight	Upset, worried
Wired	(as above), tense
Heavy	Deep, boring (confusing)
Happening	Event worth attending
Electric	Exciting, but strange
Score	To get, or to buy
Blow my cool	To get angry
Totally	More 'together' than 'together'
Together	Very confident, a good understanding
Buzz	Pleasant effect of mild stimulants (not the sound in your ears from too much listening)
Laid back	Disinterested
Mother!	(Swear word)
Cage	An institution, school, college

Tea	Marijuana (it's served in a 'joint' not out of a 'pot'. 'Pot' and 'tea' are the same, I think).
Trip	What happens to you after taking drugs
Smashed	The result of drugs, or overdoing anything
Roadie	Transportation manager (of a group, or 'band')
Dig	To be in tune with
Into	To be interested in something
To do my own thing	To establish my own set of priorities and live the way I want to live
Square	The sort of person I'm trying to avoid being, by 'doing my own thing' (at least I think that's right).

The most effective way of using such curious turns of phrase is to keep them to the minimum. Apparently this is quite acceptable and in fact the sort of youthful enthusiasm which I used to exude when I was younger is definitely not *de rigueur* among the cool.

So nowadays I stand in a corner with a bottle of brown ale in one hand and the other shoved into a pocket and let my companion do the talking, sorry, 'rapping' (or is it 'raping'? I'd advise checking that 'out' before you use it), so that all I'm called upon to do is to mutter the occasional adenoidal 'far out' or 'that's big'. Since I even developed the reputation of being quite a good conversationalist in these circles, it probably goes to show that the only real way to succeed in conversation is to let the other person do *all* the talking.

Before leaving the topic of understanding conversation, I suppose I ought to touch on the trans-Atlantic question.

This is the dilemma which has afflicted the English language ever since Paul Revere got 'booted and spurred and ready to ride' and poor old Cornwallis lost us the controlling interest in world affairs by letting George Washington win the American War of Independence.

Australians and New Zealanders live much further from these shores than the inhabitants of North America, but they manage to speak quite tolerable English, even if their manner does strike us as being rather direct. I don't mind that actually. In fact I rather like it. I've never been to Australia, or New Zealand, but my wife's got an Australian friend who came to visit us once. I'd never met him before, so I was on my best behaviour as this middle-aged man came into the room. He'd seen me in *The Good Life* in Australia so he recognized me straight away.

'How nice to meet you,' I said to him.

'Hi there, Dick,' he said, 'Where's the Scotch?'

Very direct, it broke the ice immediately.

With Americans it's different. Not that they're unfriendly – usually the reverse. But having broken away from the King, they've also broken away from the King's English. If it was a totally different language it wouldn't matter. But as with some types of jargon, so many of the words are the same that the American meanings and the British meanings can't always be distinguished.

Let me give an example.

I remember reading about an American spokesman giving a press conference in Britain on some Anglo-American project. In the course of his conversation he referred to the proposals being 'tabled'. The British press took this to mean, quite naturally, that they had been put forward for discussion, when in fact the American meant the exact opposite. In his parlance the verb 'to table' meant to shelve or postpone any discussion.

Almost any visitor to America has a story like this. That's no doubt the reason why American-British dictionaries have started to become serious reading and not just books for the loo, or Christmas stockings.

An actress friend of mine got rather tipsy with some frightfully smart American hosts on one of her earlier visits to the States. She made the careless mistake of not paying due attention to her hostess's account of her time as a (failed) young actress, before she got married, which introduced a slight chill into the conversation. Sensing this one of the others tactfully changed the subject and asked my friend how her hotel was.

'It's fine,' she said cheerfully, 'the only trouble is that I keep getting knocked up too early in the morning.'

One of those difficult pauses followed and it was only broken by the hostess leaning across and saying smugly: 'I should be rather careful how you use that expression over here, darling.'

Another word you've got to watch carefully is 'fag'. Offering someone a 'fag' over here just means offering them a cigarette. Offering someone a 'fag' in America, though, is liable to land you up in court for soliciting as a gay prostitute. You can't be too careful with your small talk anywhere from Broadstairs to Boston.

But, apparently, big talk can't be entirely relied on either. I was alarmed to hear one of the American top-level officials engaged in the SALT negotiations mention in the course of an interview that one of the biggest problems facing him was getting his point over to the Russians. That seemed obvious enough. But then he went on to say that the crucial word, the one that hangs on every statesman's lips, *détente*, did not in fact have an equivalent in Russian. Little wonder that East-West affairs have been a bit shaky in recent years.

The question remains how to smooth things over when you realize they've gone wrong. Coping with that and other emergencies is the next thing to tackle.

7

Help!

emergency conversations

Earlier I touched on various ways of getting out of ticklish spots, and there's no denying that one of the essentials of being a good conversationalist is the ability to talk your way out of any predicament. As I said before, making a bolt for it really is the last resort.

I'm not concerned here about getting away from bores, or even trying to gloss over conversational faux pas. The situations I've got in mind now fall more into the category of physical or behavioural blunders which suddenly land you in it.

I'm sure you know the sort of thing I mean. You walk into a room for an interview/to say hallo to the vicar/to meet your prospective father-in-law for an informal-man-to-man-fireside-what are your prospects and how much are you worth-chat, to find the respected gentleman smelling his armpits. You can't, or shouldn't, just stand there like a lemon, waiting for him to finish. You can't try to go out and come in again either because you're bound to have made too much noise on your way in to begin with. So what do you say?

Following my old maxim of trying to be natural, it strikes me that there's only one thing you can do and that's to come straight out with an open admission that you know exactly what he's up to and try to cure his embarrassment by saying, 'Please don't feel in the least bit put out, because as a matter of fact I'm always doing that. I reckon it's these man-made fibres they keep slipping into shirts. The way they make your hair stand on end when you pull them off is bad enough, but they never seem as comfortable as the old ones, do they? And I don't know about you, but I can't find any in my size which fit me. The arms are always too short and once they're done up to the neck I can't sit down without virtually leaning over backwards. It's hopeless trying to eat in them. The collar's so damn tight when I lean forward that I can't swallow the food. Do you have the same trouble?'

Anyone who doesn't silently thank you for that deserves to be caught off his guard. Though the worst kind of people are the ones who don't smell their armpits in private. That shows that they never think of other people. Come to think of it smelling one's armpits might not be a bad way of deciding what people are really like – a sort of acid test with a difference.

Physical complaints ought to be perfectly excusable, because they are part and parcel of being human and I defy even the most suave and *svelte* models in the glossy mags to swear on the Good Book that they've never lost their composure with a rumbling tummy or hiccups. The sad truth is that even in our permissive age these quite natural indiscretions are still regarded as *de trop*.

I've always been an appalling public speaker. I used to have terrible nerves opening fêtes and bazaars when I was younger and of course the more nervous you feel, the worse your body behaves. I used to be terrified of drying up, so I spent ages before the dreaded event learning my speech, which was fatal if I forgot what came next just as I was about to say, 'And so it is with very great pleasure that I now open the . . .' (I've got so blasé in middle-age that now I just read what I've got to say straight off a post-card if I have to. Nobody minds as long as I do open the fête, or whatever it is.)

Before I acquired this sangfroid, I did have one ghastly experience opening a charity do in a Church Hall somewhere near Maidenhead. The function was being run to raise money for some dreadful disaster which had struck the Indian sub-continent. There'd been an earthquake or a flood and these good people were

having a bazaar to send off a load of blankets and half a ton of locally-made preserved fruit to help out.

One of them had come up with the brilliant idea of combining this with an Austerity Lunch, to bring home the reality of what living in the disaster was like. If it brought it home to no one else, it brought it home to me, even if my disaster and that of the starving millions were rather different.

The catering had been organized by the formidable wife of the local lord of the manor, a lady who had been born and bred in the Punjab and who could have put down the Mutiny single-handed if she'd been given half a chance.

Now I've never flinched at trying anything once and the vegetable curry that she dished up looked pretty good, I must admit. We all queued up with bowls and spoons, and one or two who really took the whole thing terribly seriously decided to eat lunch with their fingers.

As guest of honour I was head of the queue, which in retrospect was not perhaps the wisest place to be. A great ladleful of this stuff was slopped into my bowl and I should have been warned by the burning feeling on my thumb, where she spilt a drop, that this was no ordinary curry.

I felt like the guest of honour at a Bedouin feast, tucking into the sheeps' eyes as I tentatively stirred at the brown sludge.

'Don't stand on ceremony,' bellowed the fiercesome mem-sahib, 'dig in!'

So I dug in, and in my eagerness to please accidentally swallowed a cluster of chillies that must been lying on the suface of the pot. I couldn't spit them out so I had to swallow them whole and gulp down several hasty mouthfuls in the hope that it might quieten things down.

'Jolly good show, have some more,' said the good lady and gave me another great mound of brown, steaming goo.

There wasn't much time between the end of the lunch and the opening of the bazaar. In fact I'd barely time to gulp down the last of my quart of water before I was hustled on to the stage in front of the chairs which had been piled up there to keep them out of the way.

There was so little room that the microphone they'd thoughtfully provided had to stand on the floor, which meant that it reached as high as my tum and no more. I told them that I'd manage without the microphone, but the message obviously didn't filter through to the sound boys because the thing was never switched off.

Even before I'd got going there had been the most disconcerting grumblings from my insides, which gradually rose from *pianissimo* to *fortissimo* so that by the time I started to speak I was bubbling away like a witch's cauldron. Now under normal circumstances when my stomach starts rumbling I try to carry on talking, raising my voice to hide the rumble. So I did the same this time. But the louder I talked the louder grew a sound of approaching thunder. It was a lovely day outside and I couldn't understand what was going on. So I raised my voice even higher.

Towards the end of my opening speech I was virtually shouting to make myself heard above a din of rumbles and high-pitched

squeals and whines, and I think we were all relieved when I stopped and the bazaar got under way.

'Sorry about the static,' said a pimply youth who came out from behind the curtains at the side of the stage. 'I'm afraid the amp isn't quite what you're used to with the BBC. I tried to get it as high as I could but that bloody geyser sounded as if it was going to explode by the time you finished. I'm glad someone had the sense to let off a bit of steam.'

'Oh that's alright,' I told him, trying to sound at my most jocular, 'we get the same trouble in the canteen,' which under the circumstances I regarded as rather a good reply. It was nicely ambivalent. Whether or not he, or anyone else, connected my internal upheavals with what sounded like the beginning of the storm scene in *Lear* or Macbeth's first how-d'ye-do with the three weird sisters, I never found out.

But in the car on the way home Ann commented, 'I'd dial T for Tum next time, if I were you.' And I have done ever since.

The sort of reply which is absolutely crushing is the one that doesn't offer an ounce of sympathy and makes the poor sufferer feel even worse. I'm thinking in particular of an old girl friend of mine who had the sweetest nature, but suffered from tempestuous flatulence. It was a standing joke with all her friends and once you'd got to know her she didn't make any attempt to disguise her complaint when it crept up on her.

Anyhow she was out shopping with a friend when she was taken by surprise looking in a window. She dashed after her friend, who had walked on ahead, grabbed the shoulder of his jacket and said, giggling, 'I've just done the most terrible fart.' To her horror a complete stranger turned to look at her and just said, 'Oh really' and walked on. In the circumstances I think that was somewhat heartless.

Everyone imagines that actors ought to be very good at dealing with crises of this sort, by virtue of their profession, and of course some of them are. But when things go wrong on stage it takes a very cool head to stop the audience from discovering that you're going through hell, as one friend of mine literally was when his flies burst open just after the curtain had risen on Sartre's *Huis Clos* (*In Camera*).

He'd complained to the wardrobe that his trousers were a bit dodgy, but nothing had been done about repairing them and he'd forgotten to check before he went on stage. The valet had just shown him into Hell (yes, that really is where the play is set) when he sat down and his zip ripped open from waist to crotch.

There was absolutely nothing he could do about it. He knew that he was stuck on the stage for the next hour and a bit and he knew that before too long he was going to be grappling with a very buxom actress, minus her blouse, on the settee.

If that wasn't bad enough he realized a few lines later that towards the end of the play one of the other characters would be coming out with a line that went something like, 'Now they're open – those big man's hands.' The 'hands' wouldn't make the slightest difference, he was certain. If anyone caught the line and saw the joke it would bring the house down.

So he spent the rest of the play running with sweat waiting for the line to come and hoping to God that the actress didn't dry and have to be given a prompt. She didn't, and to his intense relief the line passed unnoticed.

'Darlings, I can't thank you enough,' he told the cast when they were in the wings after the final curtain, 'I nearly died when the f***ing thing bust. I couldn't have carried on without you. I really am eternally grateful.'

'If it's your trousers you're referring to,' said one of the others, 'I think it's the most inspired bit of directing we've had in the whole production. It was a brilliant idea sending him to hell for being a flasher as well as everything else. And the way you broke out into a sweat when Estelle came on was sheer genius. I think it's us who should be thanking you.'

Now that's what I call charity.

Stumbling into intimate scenes oneself calls for just as much tact. I always wait now for an answer after knocking on a door before bursting into a room. This saves all concerned a great deal of embarrassment if there's been a little hanky-panky going on.

Exactly what you say if you do burst in to find two people violently necking depends very much on who they are in relation to you. If they're complete strangers I just say, 'Sorry, I thought this was the loo,' and quickly close the door to let them get on with it. If I know either of them, though, I've found it's easier to pretend that I was up to the same game myself, only they beat me to it in finding the best place. 'Whoops, not in here, darling,' I say over my shoulder to my imaginary accomplice, 'George has beaten us to it.'

This immediately stops my friend noticing his own guilt and makes him wonder who on earth I was with. If he asks later, I just say, 'You keep my secret, chum, and I'll keep yours,' and it always works.

Compromising situations do call for a cool head, there's no denying it. You don't even need to be in the wrong to be branded guilty; you need merely say the wrong thing at the wrong time. The police in particular tend to be very suspicious if they catch us doing anything out of the ordinary.

One of my friends had just bought a new car and had treated himself to a sun-roof, which he'd always wanted. He had been rehearsing until the early hours of the morning and on his way home he stopped off to post a couple of letters at the main sorting office, so that they would be delivered that day.

When he got out of the car he didn't bother to switch off the engine, since he was only going to be out of it for a second or two. He hadn't fully mastered the locks on the doors, however, and to his horror he tried to open the driver's door to find that it had locked itself. All the other doors had locked as well and he was left standing in the street at three in the morning with the engine running, the headlights on full beam and absolutely no way of getting inside.

He cursed his luck, kicked the hub-plate, which fell off, and trudged off to find a phone-box so that he could ring the AA.

It took him some time to find one and by the time he had made his call he realized that the battery must be running down. So he raced back and had one final go at trying all the locks. It was still no use. He had finally resolved to wait until the breakdown van came to help him out when he caught sight of the sun-roof and an idea came to him.

He was so pleased with his brainwave that he didn't hear the policeman's measured footsteps as he was forcing open the sun-roof.

'Good morning, sir. Having a little trouble are we?'

'Yes, as a matter of fact I am, officer,' my friend told him, 'I've stupidly locked myself out.'

'And how did you come to do that, may I ask?'

'I was posting some letters.'

'Posting some letters,' said the policeman slowly as he wrote in his little book.

'Would you mind telling me the number of this vehicle sir?'

'No. W, F, C . . . no, F, C, W, . . . wait a minute it's C, W, F, . . . Well, to be quite honest I can't remember off-hand. I've only just bought the car you see.'

'Only just bought the car,' said the policeman as he wrote that down in his book. 'It doesn't seem to be your night does it, sir.'

'No, I don't suppose it does,' said my friend starting to feel a bit sheepish.

'Would you mind telling me where you've been this evening?'

'At work. I've been working.'

'At work,' muttered the policeman. 'And what do you do that keeps you up at this hour of the morning?'

'I'm an actor,' said my friend.

'An actor, are you now? I don't suppose this has anything to do with your work does it?' said the policeman wryly, but giving my chum an idea.

'Well since you ask, it does,' he said, 'But the producer will kill me if you let on to anyone. It's part of a new series on the box and we've been scratching our heads wondering how I could break into a car that's been left like this. You see the series starts with this abandoned car in the middle of the country in the dead of night. It's terribly dramatic. But please, it would be more than my life's worth if you let out what I've told you.'

'Why didn't you say so to begin with?' asked the policeman tearing the page out of his little book. 'You don't want to go messing about on the roof like that. Any fool in the business knows this is how you do it,' and he took a piece of wire from his pocket, fiddled about with the lock and the door was open in a flash. 'I'm always having to open doors when damn fool drivers go and lose their keys, though some of them even go and ring up the AA, bloody idiots,' he said. 'And another thing, sir. Remember it's best to come out with the truth straight away. All that nonsense about posting letters, you don't honestly expect me to believe that, at this time of night.'

'No, I suppose not,' said my chum as he drove off, passing the AA van that was arriving to help him.

Brushes with the law are always unnerving, particularly if we're completely innocent of the charge, and the people I really admire are those who have the presence of mind to turn false accusations to their advantage.

My mother once told me the story of a tremendous coup pulled by a shopper in a really smart West End shop. She'd been dragged in by one of the store detectives accused of stealing a head-scarf. She knew perfectly well that she'd been wearing the thing when she came in and that it had a label from a shop in Belgium where she'd bought it on holiday the year before.

However, instead of pleading her innocence there and then and convincing them that she couldn't have taken it, she demanded to have her solicitor present and also told them to call the police. All this took some time and when the police car appeared outside the shop it caused quite a commotion (there must have been fewer shop-lifters then than there are today). The policeman asked the store-detective what had happened and he said that he had seen the woman try on the scarf, appear to put it down and then go into the Ladies. But when he checked, he found that the scarf he'd seen was missing. 'And it's the one she's wearing,' he concluded, pointing to the one from Brussels.

'Do you wish to say anything, madam,' asked the policeman.

'Yes, would the manager promise me he would settle out of court, if I'm guilty?'

'This is a criminal matter, I'm afraid,' said the policeman, 'It'll have to go to court.'

'And we always prosecute,' added the manager, smugly.

'In that case would you be kind enough, officer, to note that this scarf has the label of a shop on the continent, in which I bought it a year ago. And would you also note that I intend to instruct my solicitor to take out proceedings against this shop.'

They were all rather taken aback and the manager blushingly acknowledged that there must have been some mistake.

'Would madam consider choosing one of our wide range of scarves by way of an apology, if we forget the whole affair?'

'No, I wouldn't,' replied the lady, 'But I'll take a grand piano. Here's my address.'

Mother was green with envy. She tried it once but no one took any notice of her lifting things off various counters and in the end she gave up.

Most of the instances I mentioned above are one-offs, at least one hopes they are. But there are awkward moments that have a habit of rearing their heads more than once and the most effective way of dealing with them is to have a variety of ready-made excuses tucked up our sleeves. If they work once, there's no reason why, perhaps with a little modification, they shouldn't work time and time again.

A good example of this was the actor whose run of luck was so bad that he eventually gave up looking for parts and took to driving a mini-cab instead. He was pretty humiliated by this and did all he could to disguise himself with five o'clock shadow and a flat cap.

But one day when he was stuck in a line of traffic he saw an old

flame walking along the pavement. He knew that she was appearing in a very successful West End show and from her appearance he could see that she was clearly doing very well. He made the mistake of staring at her for far too long, because she caught his eye and recognized him, which was the last thing he wanted. He couldn't make a move when she walked over to him to say 'hello', so he beckoned her out of the way and hissed, 'Piss off, you're in the camera shot.' He was so pleased with this that he used it on all his friends after that. But the funny thing was that after a while word got about that he was doing so much filming that he was finally offered a real job back on the boards, which bucked him up no end.

Many of the most inventive excuses that I've come across have been connected with work in one way or another. Whether it's been a case of explaining to a furious client why his order is four weeks overdue or getting off work to attend a relation's funeral, which just so happens to coincide with the Varsity Match, the mind of the working man seems to lack nothing in imagination or quick wits.

The story of the office junior taking the day off work to go to his father-in-law's funeral is a good example. A young chap had convinced his boss that he couldn't possibly avoid going to the funeral, in spite of the fact that the firm was up to its eyes with work. So he might have been expected to show some signs of guilt when he was confronted by his boss at a major cup-tie replay that same afternoon.

'So this is your father-in-law's funeral,' said the boss knowingly.

'It will be in a minute,' said the clerk without a moment's hesitation, 'He's the referee.'

Businessmen come out with some wonderful lines when they're up against it, too. When trying to disguise that their work force has gone on strike yet again they'll tell their clients, 'We can't guarantee delivery before two months because we're facing a greater pile-up of work than we've ever known before.'

Or they'll try to explain the all-too evident lack of activity with, 'Yes, it's one of our most forward-thinking ideas. Give the work force their annual holiday when everyone else is hard at it. It gives them the pick of the resorts. It helps them get cut-price holidays, and it makes them feel that little bit special. This is only the first year we've tried it, but you can see for yourself how splendidly it's going.'

Cash flow and other financial difficulties must be the rule rather than the exception these days so the excuses must be running pretty thin. The point in the businessman's favour is that everyone knows how tight things are and in many cases all he has to do is to mutter 'interest rates' or 'the high value of the pound' and he gets away with another fortnight's credit.

'We're just getting used to the new computer in the accounts department. These things always have teething troubles. I'll get on to your account straight away and make sure that the money is dispatched immediately,' is usually good enough to drag out non-payment for a further week, especially as the Post Office further plays into our hands. Most businessmen can quote at least one example of a letter taking three weeks to get from Wolverhampton to West Bromwich.

Punctuality can be covered by similar external factors – 'God, I'm sorry I'm so late – good thing you got going before I arrived. They cancelled all the trains on the Central Line for half an hour and left us stuck in the tunnel between Edgware Road and Baker Street. You can't imagine what I said to the station manager by the time I got out.'

Cheek has it's part to play in excuses for lateness, too. Charles Lamb almost made it a point of principle never to arrive on time at his office and when he was finally reprimanded by his immediate superior saying, 'You arrive very late, Mr Lamb,' he calmly answered him, 'Yes, but notice how early I leave.'

That elegance of phrase has all but disappeared today, but the spirit is still alive in many offices and factories:

'You've been late every morning for the last fortnight,' one employee was chillingly informed by his boss,' What have you got to say about it?'

'That I am consistent in everything I do, sir,' he replied.

Many people would agree that the most vital excuses are the ones that save marriages, or at least save one half of a marriage. These, I find, tend to cover two main areas of transgression – taking the other half for granted, and misbehaviour.

The first is usually linked with forgetfulness, and high on the list of things to be forgotten are birthdays and anniversaries. In spite of my natural absent-mindedness, fate has always smiled on me in this respect and I've never forgotten our wedding anniversary.

I've learned not to be too cocky about this, though. One fellow came horribly unstuck by flaunting similar good luck while he and his wife were enjoying their eighteenth wedding anniversary dinner. She congratulated him on his flawless record. He'd never forgotten to send her flowers or arrange a lovely treat for that special day.

'It's simple,' he explained, his tongue loosened with wine, 'We got married on Samantha's birthday.'

'Oh well, that would explain it,' she said coldly. 'And who is Samantha, by the way?'

In actual fact there is no excuse for forgetting the date of one's marriage, but the most effective means of wriggling out of having forgotten to send a card, for instance, is to admit to not having sent one on purpose, because instead you've arranged a really special surprise for this particular anniversary.

'I chanced running the risk of putting your back up, my love, because I wanted this to be a really special event. Go and pack an overnight bag while I just arrange the taxi,' is a suitably enigmatic line that gives you enough breathing space to check your bank balance and decide which hotel to ring and book a room in. Then you cross your fingers and hope they've got a vacancy. If they have, arrange for flowers and champagne to be waiting for you and dictate a note to be typed by the receptionist and left on the flowers. Then ring the office and leave a message to say that you won't be in tomorrow. Then ring for a taxi to take you both to the hotel.

Mind you, if you can afford to go a little further afield it's infinitely better to drive in your own car. It saves money and you can always say you thought it would be much more like going away on honeymoon again.

Forgetting wedding anniversaries can cause terrible scenes at the time, but they're not nearly as bad as the smouldering rage which follows the discovery of some misbehaviour, by which I mean a little bit on the side.

The tell-tale lipstick on the collar has always struck me as being a grossly overrated problem, providing that you usually travel to work on some form of crowded commuter transport. I don't see any reason why you shouldn't say, 'I didn't even notice it until now. It's such a crush in that blasted train that I'm not surprised someone's head pushed into me. I spent the whole journey back with my nose pressed up against a head as bald as Kojak's. It was like being a mouse and looking a billiard ball in the eye.'

No, the real time to start worrying is when you're actually caught red-handed, so to speak. You can try to introduce your lady friend as a colleague who's just joined the firm/a client/the boss's daughter/a market researcher/a reporter who's doing an article on the business – but only if the circumstances seem likely. None of those would be the slightest use if you were seen by a friend with the lady in a compromising position in a cinema or disco.

Under those circumstances you'd have to try something like, 'What am I doing here? Isn't it obvious? I'm doing the background work on the new line we're planning for next autumn. But I don't know the first thing about what's needed, so this young lady has kindly agreed to help me. "You need to get with it, if the thing's going to take off", the old man said. So that's just what I'm doing.'

If it's your wife, on the other hand, who catches you kissing your secretary at the office party you could always try a line I once overheard in a pub, 'I wasn't kissing her. I was just whispering into her mouth.'

Drink is the other major hazard faced by the married man, and if it's accompanied by having had a good time out, while the wife has been stuck at home, the reception is usually pretty frosty.

I don't go out with the lads anymore. I used to go to pubs quite a lot, but now that it costs you about £72 for a round of drinks I prefer to drink at home. This means that I'm seldom faced with the prospect of waking my wife at one in the morning to be asked why I've lost my key and why I'm pickled. There's not a lot you can say if you really are one over the eight, or more to the point there's not a lot you should say. But there was one chap I heard of who had what I consider to be an absolutely cast-iron excuse.

His wife let him in wearing her dressing gown and looking daggers. 'What have you got to say for yourself?' she asked icily.

'Nothing, dear,' he told her sheepishly, 'Except that I had to get this drunk.'

'What do you mean, you had to.'

'Well, you know that you're always telling me that I can't take too much booze because it's against the law? I remembered this as I finished the second pint, which as you are always telling me, too, is more than enough. I was terrified that I might be breathalyzed and lose my licence, so I decided that the only sure way out was to get more sozzled than any of the others so that I would be the last person who'd have to drive back. And I was. I hope you understand.'

This excuse starts to lose its effectiveness with more than one telling. But once is better than never.

.   .   .

On the subject of domestic and family excuses I find keeping my end up with the kids can be quite an uphill struggle at times. It's their school work which gets me into a state more than anything else.

Helping a child with the answers to his homework these days is very difficult, if like me you can't understand the questions. I used to try telling them, 'You know I'd like to help you, but do you think I really should? I mean the teachers set you the homework didn't they? They know that *I* can do it. What they want to find out is whether *you* can.'

But that, too, started to wear a bit thin, so then I tried to suggest that it wasn't that I couldn't do the prep, it was just that I didn't want to confuse them with old-fashioned ideas and methods. But that didn't cut much ice either. In the end I gave up trying and advised them that they'd be better off asking their mother, who was much more intelligent than their father.

The children's chance confrontations with sex can bring a few blushes to one's cheeks, too, until you eventually summon up enough courage to face the most awkward chat of your life.

Sometimes having a dog can be more of a handicap than one might imagine if the kids catch sight of it *in flagrante delicto*. This, I hasten to add, has never been the case with ours. Paddy has always behaved like a perfect gentleman, in public at any rate. But we've been out for a walk in the park sometimes and heard inquisitive children ask their horrified parents, 'Daddy, what's Humphrey doing with that doggie?' What does one say? One impressively quick-witted dad answered, 'He's helping it along. The other dog's very old and can't see very well so Humphrey's helping her . . . er . . . it to find the gate. That's why he's pushing it along . . . Come along now, Humphrey. I think she's got the idea . . . Humphrey!'

Following the chat about the facts of life the only other help a parent can give his offspring is warning them about being led astray, or at least warning them about when and when not to try to lead anyone astray. I suppose it's still inevitable that girls will be more at risk in this respect, certainly when they start going out with boyfriends, and a few helpful lines to get them out of any near scrapes without putting the chap off completely ought to be in every caring parent's note-book:

No, I'm not in the mood.

I don't know you well enough.

I think if we wait you'll see that I'm interested in you as more than just a one-night stand.

Him: Surely you know that a man can't go for more than two days without sex.
Her: Bye, then. I'll see you in a couple of days time.

Him: Why don't you and I go for a walk in the moonlight alone?
Her: Why don't you go for a walk in the moonlight alone?

Him: Tonight's perfect. If we do it now nothing will be different between us tomorrow.
Her: If nothing's going to be different tomorrow, why don't we just leave it as it is now?

Him: If I told you you've got a fabulous figure would you hold it against me?
Her: No, I wouldn't, because I've always believed that first impressions can sometimes be conceiving.

Him: I don't see any reason why we shouldn't go to bed with each other. Everyone else does.
Her: That's fine isn't it. You won't have much trouble then in finding someone to help you out.

It could be argued, however, that in the present climate of law and order our kids would be of more help to us in preparing a list of suitable phrases and exhortations to give their poor old parents to prevent them from being mugged on the way down to Waitrose or the bookies.

Which really brings me to my last point, which I suppose paradoxically should be at the beginning, if it didn't spell the end – if you see what I mean.

8

The Last Word

If it's true that our children learn to speak by listening to what we say and imitating our sounds, it's worth bearing in mind that everything we say during their crucial formative years will have some bearing on their development as conversationalists.

HE'S JUST GOT STUMPED FOR HIS FIRST WORD

I'm not suggesting that we should go around spouting Johnson, or any other favoured conversationalist, but it is worth remembering that every muffled curse, every foul expletive, every vicious name and snide retort that passes our lips, will sooner or later filter through to their little brains to be blurted back at us sometime in the future as they make their first tentative steps in conversation.

There's no point shouting, 'I don't want to hear you using that word ever again', because the chances are that they picked it up from us in the first place, and they're certainly going to hear it from us again before they're very much older.

But pause here for a moment's thought. 'The child is father of the man', wrote Wordsworth.

Perhaps, if he's right, we'd all be better off communicating in baby talk (it's amazing how many adults already seem to take to it so easily). After all, babies seem to get along perfectly well.

Though for that matter, what about animals? If brute beasts can lead contented, uncomplicated lives without recourse to conversation, or even speech, could it not be that it is we who have been barking up the wrong tree for the last few millenia?

> Ye blessed creatures, I have heard the call
> Ye to each other make; I see
> The heavens laugh with you in your jubilee

wrote Wordsworth, too. Now few would deny that he had a way with words. His name as good as tells us. So if he got the message, communing with nature as he did, maybe our sedentary, urban existence, in fact all the trappings of what we call civilization, is going in the wrong direction?

We set such importance against becoming accomplished conversationalists that we often cloud the real importance of communication. In other words, in spite of what I've said about the guile, art, craft, skill, deception, fraud, secrecy and entertainment we find in conversation, it's the simple ability to communicate which really matters in the end. Don't you agree?